Readings for Lent and Easter

From The Upper Room

Readings for Lent and Easter

Cover Design: Cindy Helms
Cover photograph: Byron Jorjorian
First Printing: January 1993 (10)
Library of Congress Catalog Card Number: 92-61444
ISBN: 0-8358-0681-2

Printed in the United States of America

CONTENTS

PREFACE   9

Week One: A Time of Preparation
   Day 1: Final Sanity   13
      Phyllis A. Tickle
   Day 2: I Need Renewal   15
      Kenneth G. Phifer
   Day 3: Entering the Wilderness   17
      Larry R. Kalajainen
   Day 4: I Would Be a Saint   20
      Wanda M. Trawick
   Day 5: Quest for the Savior   22
      Bill Bates
   Day 6: Close to God's Heart   23
      Rueben P. Job
   Day 7: The Story Continues   24
      Anne Broyles

Week Two: To Forgive and Be Forgiven
   Day 8: Mercy and Judgment in God's Realm   29
      K. Cherie Jones
   Day 9: I Turn to You   31
      Kenneth G. Phifer
   Day 10: Redemption   34
      Carole F. Chase
   Day 11: Winners and Losers   36
      Helen R. Neinast and Thomas C. Ettinger
   Day 12: Our Anger and God's Heart   38
      Flora Slosson Wuellner
   Day 13: But Could I Do It 489 More Times?   41
      Mary Montgomery

Day 14: Forgiveness   45
    Pixie Koestline Hammond

Week Three: Here Is Joy, Here Is Hope

Day 15: Celebration Beyond Tears   49
    J. Barrie Shepherd
Day 16: A Little Madness   52
    Maxie Dunnam
Day 17: The Story of Anna White   54
    Marilyn Wickel
Day 18: Christ Comes Running   56
    Jim Frisbie
Day 19: Prepare to Celebrate!   57
    Donald E. Collins
Day 20: The Stations of the Cross   58
    Parker J. Palmer
Day 21: Running to God   60
    Roger Pierce

Week Four: Turning Toward God

Day 22: Journey without End   63
    Beth A. Richardson
Day 23: Shadowbound   64
    David M. Griebner
Day 24: Standing in God's Presence   67
    Catherine Gunsalus González
    The Crux   68
    Lois Duffield
Day 25: Do I Have to Take Him with Me?   69
    Richard Whitaker
Day 26: Intuition of Wholeness   72
    John S. Mogabgab
Day 27: Saying Goodbyes   74
    Richard L. Morgan
Day 28: Daily Dancing with the Holy One   75
    Jean M. Blomquist

Week Five: Love Beyond Understanding

    Day 29: God's Covenant Love   81
        Linda M. Small

    Day 30: I Am Not Sure of Love   83
        Kenneth G. Phifer

    Day 31: Sam's No-Hit, No-Run Game   85
        Gerry H. Moore

    Day 32: On Friendship   91
        David G. Broadbent

    Day 33: Compassion and Commitment   92
        Gustavo Gutiérrez

    Day 34: Miniature   94
        Dorothy Hanson Brown

    Day 35: Remember Who You Are   95
        William H. Willimon

Week Six: Times of Trial

    Day 36: A Way to Remember   101
        Nola M. Sorrells

    Day 37: Out of the Depths   102
        Donald E. Collins

    Day 38: Of Seeds and Suffering   104
        Jean M. Blomquist

    Day 39: Rabbits in Winter   106
        Donna Schaper

    Day 40: When Loneliness Does Not Go Away   108
        Donald J. Shelby

    Day 41: Midnight Invocation   111
        Barbara Seaman

        Jesus Struggles with Us   111
        James A. Harnish

    Day 42: Un Sacrificio de Amor   113
        (A Sacrifice of Love)
        Palmira S. Oliveras

Week Seven: Through the Darkness into the Light

Day 43: Judas Iscariot   119
       Mary Lou Redding
Day 44: Not Servants But Friends   121
       Barbara Brown Taylor
Day 45: 40 Days   125
       Ken Fansler
       Good Friday   125
       Larry R. Kalajainen
Day 46: The Heart of Christian Paradox   127
       Marjorie J. Thompson
Day 47 (Easter): Easter Morning   129
       Kefa Sempangi
       An Easter Litany   134
       Michael E. Williams
       The Women   135
       Kenneth L. Gibble
After Easter: Our Own Galilee   136
       Dan Moore
Putting on Christ   137
       Ron DelBene
Come   140
       Thomas John Carlisle

QUESTIONS FOR DISCUSSION   143
ABOUT THE AUTHORS   153

PREFACE

The rhythm of the church year reflects the rhythm of the spiritual life. Lent is a quiet, reflective season of the heart, a time to look inward in order that we might look Godward.

It is often difficult to resist the pace of contemporary life, the demands of work and family and commitment to friends and worthy tasks. But for forty days during Lent, we are called to spend soul time searching once again for the centerline on our journey with and toward God. In the shadow of the Cross, we confess our sins and express our agonies. With the assurance of the Resurrection, we claim our joys and celebrate our blessings.

In *Readings for Lent and Easter,* we offer meditations, essays, poems, and excerpts to nurture and sustain your search. The readings have been selected from all the publication areas of The Upper Room: *Weavings, The Upper Room Daily Devotional Guide, alive now!, Pockets, El Aposento Alto,* and selected Upper Room books.

These readings have been grouped thematically so that they may also be used for small group discussion. Questions for reflection (on page 143) will assist group leaders who wish to use the book in this way.

We encourage you to accept the gift that Lent can be in your life. Take time to reconsider what is essential. Take time to search for God, who is, even now, searching for you.

THE EDITORS

Week One

A Time of Preparation

Create in me a clean heart,
  O God,
and put a new and right
  spirit within me.
                    Psalm 51:10

We entreat you on behalf of Christ, be reconciled to God.
For our sake he made him to be sin who knew no sin, so
that in him we might become the righteousness of God.
                    2 Corinthians 5:20-21

FINAL SANITY

enzin, our German ancestors used to call this season, and since then we have called it "Lent." It is a time when Christians decorate stone churches with the sea's color and wrap their priests in the mollusk's purple. It was once a time when all things passed through the natural depression of seclusion, short food supplies, and inactivity, a time when body and land both rested. It is still, in the country, a final sanity before the absurd wastefulness of spring.

Each year at this time it is harder for me to desire butterflies and lilies, even to wish for resurrection. Each year I come a little closer to needing the dullness of the sky and the rarity of a single redheaded woodpecker knocking for grubs in my pine bark. Each year also I come a little closer to the single-mindedness of the drake who, muddy underside showing, waddles now across the ice to the cold center water to wash himself for his mate, all in the hope of ducklings later on.

Through the thin sharp air I can hear the younger children in the barn. They are building tunnels again, making forts from the dried bales of hay. From the yapping I know that even the dogs can join in the intricacies which imagination has contrived. The five-year-old chases field mice as her brothers build. She will catch another soon and drown it in the water trough with unsullied sadism, feeling only the accomplishment that comes from having helped to keep her part of the world in balance.

In the summer, the mice will leave, going back to the fields again, and she will take to pulling everything that blooms instead, bringing them all in to me indiscriminately. The tin-roofed barn will be stifling, and the forts will have all been eaten. The boys will be picking beans and complaining of the itch from the okra leaves, being themselves too hot and tired to desire anything except nightfall and bed. The drake will have a family, which he will abandon to the mate he so much desires now, and the woodpecker's carmine head will burn out to tired tan. The farm in the summer becomes like the city is all year . . . too much color, too much noise, too much growing, too much hurry to stave off loss and destruction, too little natural death and gentle ending, too little time for play, too little pointless imagination.

I can remember many summers now; it is the singular advantage of years that one can do so. And I remember that once summer comes, I spend it wallowing in the easiness of it; the excess of its fruits and vegetables, the companionship of its constant sounds as the hum of the insects and of the Rototillers gives way in the evening to the croaking of the frogs and the raucousness of the katydids. I remember also that I begin early, in that green time of Trinity, to dread the stillness of the coming cold; to fear the weariness of winter menus, the bitterness of breaking open pond water for thirsty cattle and of packing lunches—interminable lunches—for reluctant children on their way to school.

But for right now it is Lent and for one more snow I can luxuriate in the isolation of the cold, attend laconically to who I am and what I value and why I'm here. Religion has always kept earth time. Liturgy only gives sanction to what the heart already knows.

—Phyllis A. Tickle
Final Sanity

I NEED RENEWAL

O Lord our God,
You have given me the gift of life,
and when I abuse it you restore me
that I may try again.
You are both a conservationist and a restorationist.
You work with me to conserve that which I never quite lose,
  the sense of the holiness of life
    that I never quite obliterate,
  the reverence I feel at least occasionally,
  and the wonder I know now and again.
Your Spirit works within
    to deepen and broaden my appreciation
      for the gift of life,
    and I am grateful.
When left to myself,
  I confess I grow careless and blunder along,
    bumping into other people and jostling them aside,
    stomping on flowers and tromping across the grass.
I forget to pray and neglect praise.
But you keep working within me,
    making me restless in my boorishness
    and discontented with my clumsy handling of life.
Deliver me from ever settling down,
    satisfied in rude rejection of love and faith and hope.

Restore me, I pray, for I need restoration.
I do not ask to be put back into the shape I once was.
I know that the very experiences that have marred me,
    even scarred me,
    and have given my life its weather-beaten quality,

are the experiences by which I have grown and learned.
I pray that I may be refurbished within,
    that my mind may be refurnished,
    and my heart redecorated
        with joy and gladness. Amen.

—Kenneth G. Phifer
A Book of Uncommon Prayer

Day 3

ENTERING THE WILDERNESS

*R*ead Mark 1:1-13.
Reflect for a few moments on the meaning of *wilderness* for Mark. It is the place where people go to express their repentance. It is the place of Jesus' anointing and commission. It is the place where Jesus is tested for forty days. It is in the wilderness that Jesus is ministered to by angels.

Forty is an important symbolic number. In the story of Noah, the rain lasted forty days and forty nights, Moses was forty days on Mt. Sinai, Israel wandered forty years in the wilderness, Elijah was sustained forty days in the wilderness when he fled from Ahab, and Jonah announced that Nineveh would be overthrown in forty days. The church's observance of the forty days of Lent (Sundays excepted, as they are feast days in Lent) is a recognition of the importance of the number *forty* in scripture and of the wilderness experience—both of Jesus and of those who are called to follow him.

What wilderness experiences have you known in your life? When have you been aware you were being tested for some future work? Have you felt the sense of loneliness that the word *wilderness* conjures up? Describe that loneliness. Is it possible that the wilderness can be both a place where we face testing, fear, and loneliness, and a place where we are strengthened and renewed for mission?

As you read the Gospel of Mark, notice places where Jesus withdraws to the wilderness or "a lonely place" and what happens at those times.

[Lent] is a time for repentance. Look within yourself and allow God's spirit to point out to you those habits, attitudes, and behaviors which may be blocking you from a deeper walk with God. You may wish to write these down. Writing can help us to be truthful with ourselves. When you have named those roadblocks which hinder your journey, ask for and receive God's forgiveness.

Out of the teachings of Abba Isaac, a desert father of the fourth century, comes a meditation formula for "descending with the mind into the heart," a common expression for withdrawing from distractions and centering oneself in God's presence. Begin with this verse from Psalm 40:13 (early translation): "O God, come to my assistance; O Lord, make haste to help me." In *Centering Prayer* Basil Pennington cites Abba Isaac's own words on this verse,

> Rightly has this verse been selected from the whole Bible to serve this purpose. It suits every mood and temper of human nature, every temptation, every circumstance. It contains an invocation of God, a humble confession of faith, a reverent watchfulness, a meditation on human frailty, an act of confidence in God's response, an assurance of ever-present support. The [person] who continually invokes God as his [or her] protector is aware that God is ever at hand.

Spend two or three minutes repeating this prayer silently. While praying, breathe deeply and rhythmically, perhaps saying the first phrase of the prayer while inhaling and the second phrase while exhaling. Remember, the point is to focus attention not on the prayer itself or on your bodily state but on God.

While you are aware of being in God's presence, lift up to God your concerns for others. You may name these persons or simply imagine them being in the Divine Presence, where God's perfect knowledge of them meets their needs.

Conclude the time of prayer by slowly and thoughtfully praying the Lord's Prayer.

As you go about your daily routine, look around you and consciously attempt to "read" God's revelation in the world around you. Also, use the prayer "O God, come to my assistance; O Lord, make haste to help me" at frequent intervals throughout the day—while driving or while preparing dinner, for example. The point of this exercise is to increase your attentiveness to God amid the ordinary activities of everyday life.

Let people and events of your day call you to lift them into the presence of God as you seek to be attentive to that presence.

—Larry R. Kalajainen
A Lenten Journey

I WOULD BE A SAINT

*A*bout 300 years ago, there lived a great man called Brother Lawrence. He lived in a monastery where he worked as a cook for the others who lived there. He discovered that all the time he was cooking and working in the monastery he could think about God. He thought about God's being with him, and he told God all the things he was thinking. He called this "practicing the presence of God." He believed that we can get to know God better when we think about God's being with us wherever we are.

Lots of times, when we think about prayer, we think about the prayers that we say. We say the Lord's Prayer, or we say a prayer thanking God for our food before we eat, or we say a prayer before we go to bed at night. Sometimes we stop what we are doing and say a prayer about something special.

But Brother Lawrence taught us that there are other ways to pray, too. He taught that all through the day we can know that God is with us, and we can be praying all the time. That may sound strange, but we are praying when we say "thank you" silently when God helps us get through a hard test. Or we can silently say "please help me, God" when we are afraid. Without anyone else hearing, we can say "I love you, God" when we think of the wonderful world God has given us. We don't even have to say silent words.

If we are aware that God is with us, that is praying, too. On the school playground, or at the park, or playing with a friend—anytime at all—you can know that God is with you. It is part of our adventure of getting to know God!

—Staff
Pockets

I would be like that "kitchen saint,"
who among the pots and pans
"practiced the presence of God"
while meeting each day's demands.
Like Brother Lawrence, I would learn
that God is with me when I play,
when I study, and when I work,
not only when I pray.
And I would learn that every labor
is done for God as well as neighbor.

—Wanda M. Trawick
Pockets

QUEST FOR THE SAVIOR

*R*ead John 12:20-26.

The temptation is to skip past those curious Greeks who wanted to meet Jesus and get on to his important message. And yet, their quest for Jesus seems to be the triggering event for the glorifying of Christ. Time and again Jesus had said, "The hour has not yet come" (John 2:4; 7:6, 30; 8:20). But now he says, "The hour has come for the Son of man to be glorified."

Was it that now Jesus could see that his handful of followers would not remain a tiny Jewish sect? Could he see past a few Greeks to untold millions of Gentiles who would seek him in the future?

"We wish to see Jesus," they said. Is that not even now the beginning point for faith? And because we start at that point, does he not still say, "Now the hour has come."

In the scripture passage, at first it seems that Jesus is not answering the request. Gradually, an awareness grows that here is how to conduct our quest for the Savior.

He says that when we are ready to die to ourselves like the single seed in the fertile soil, which dies and becomes fruitful, then we will see him. When we begin to love life in his kingdom more than we love a self-centered, self-serving existence, then we will see him and be honored by our Creator.

We dare not ignore those Greek seekers because they are you and I.

Prayer: *We wish to see you, Jesus. Amen.*

—Bill Bates
The Upper Room Disciplines 1985

CLOSE TO GOD'S HEART

O ur first grandchild has arrived, and he is wonderful! It has been amazing to me how quickly and clearly he has declared that his favorite position is upright and held closely to the heart. Perhaps it's the warmth, the security of strong arms, or perhaps the sound and pressure of a beating heart that reminds him of his maternal home and draws him to this position. At any rate, upright, and close to the heart, he coos, smiles, sleeps, and observes and experiences the world in contentment and security.

When I push myself away from God or simply permit myself to drift away from God, loneliness and a sense of abandonment can overtake me quickly and easily. But when I hear and heed God's call, try to press close to God's heart, I, too, experience the world and all of its uncertainty with a new measure of serenity and security.

—Rueben P. Job
alive now!

W e forget that we too are children whose hearts must be opened, trusting and needful of God's deep embrace where all joy, all suffering is felt and borne.

—Wendy M. Wright
Weavings

Day 7

THE STORY CONTINUES

*O*ne way to deeply interact with the word of God in a formational way is to read a scripture passage and then journal in response to the word. The act of journaling brings about an intimate relationship between the reader-journaler and the biblical story. The reader is pulled from informational "head-reading" to formational interaction: What is the word of God specifically saying to me?

The Bible has been guiding God-seeking people throughout the centuries. Individuals have found different verses or stories to be helpful to them in their spiritual pilgrimages. The Bible can be most formational when viewed as a continuing story. Old Testament books narrate the story of the people of Israel and their relationship to God. The New Testament tells of the life of Jesus and how his resurrection affected the early church. And the love story of God and humanity does not end with the last page of the Bible. God is ever-creating, ever-interacting in today's world as well—the story continues.

One of the characters in *The Winter of Our Discontent* by John Steinbeck knew the power of the continuing God-story in her life. Aunt Deborah "read the Scripture to me like a daily newspaper and I suppose that's the way she thought of it, as something going on happening eternally but always exciting and new. Every Easter, Jesus really rose from the dead, an explosion, expected but nonetheless new. It wasn't two thousand years ago to her; it was now."

How is Jesus' resurrection affecting your present life? How does the biblical story interact with your own story (past, present, and future)? Journaling can help you focus on questions such as these that apply to you even as they applied to Abraham, Esther, Mary Magdalene, Paul, and Christians throughout the centuries.

Here is an opportunity to try journaling in response to scripture. There is a scripture passage to experience, then some questions to begin the journaling process. As you read, remember that the goal is not to read a certain amount of words from the Bible or to analyze all the meanings of the text. The goal of journaling with scripture is to understand the word of God as it intimately relates to you . . . take time to let God speak to you through that verse. It might be a window to your relationship with the Divine Mystery, bringing you closer to God this day.

God Transforms Our Weakness (Luke 13:10-17)
Immediately she was made straight, and she praised God.

—Luke 13:13

Before reading the scripture passage, spend three minutes walking around bent over in half. Imagine yourself talking to people you meet on the street. How does it feel to relate to others from this stance? Can you imagine always looking down instead of up?

When the three minutes are up, do some stretches to relax your back. Stand straight and stretch to the sky. Then bend forward until your head is hanging relaxed to the floor. Feel the strength of a healthy back before relaxing into your time of journaling.

If physical restrictions make it impossible for you to take the three minutes of bent-over time, close your eyes and visualize yourself in that position. Perhaps your own restrictions will be a gift to you in understanding this passage.

After reading the verses of scripture, consider these questions:

1. Think of the woman who spent eighteen years bent over in a spirit of infirmity. How was her vision

narrowed? What possibilities would have been closed to her?

2. When Jesus responds to the remarks of the ruler of the synagogue (v.16), what is he saying about the worth of this woman?

3. Many things can bend one's back: loneliness, injustice, hopelessness, resentment, oppression, despair. In your own life, what is it that causes your back to bend? How would you identify the bent-over part of yourself? What might be your spirit of infirmity?

4. In your journal, write a prayer to Jesus, detailing your own infirmity (weakness, failing). Share your feelings honestly, knowing that you will be heard. Take a few moments of silence. Then write what Jesus might say to you, as he said to the woman bent over for eighteen years: "Woman, you are freed from your frailty."

—Anne Broyles
Journaling: A Spirit Journey

Week Two

To Forgive and Be Forgiven

Happy are those whose
transgression is forgiven,
whose sin is covered.
                    Psalm 32:1

Just as by the one man's disobedience the many were made
sinners, so by the one man's obedience the many will be
made righteous.
                                    Romans 5:19

MERCY AND JUDGMENT IN GOD'S REALM

*R*ead Luke 13:1-5.

In the prime of his life, Dale was diagnosed as having a rare form of cancer. Several months later his wife, Pam, was asked if they had ever questioned why he had contracted this disease. Her response was that as Christians they both knew they were not exempt from suffering. They did not assume that this disease was a punishment for some sin on Dale's part. And they knew that God loves them. Their faith is empowering them to deal with this illness.

Their attitude stands in stark contrast to the attitudes of so many of us who look for cause-and-effect relationships to explain why bad things happen to people. "Surely," we reason, "she must have done something to deserve this misfortune." "Surely he must have sinned some horrible sin to account for this traumatic occurrence." And so we attempt to find meaning when an infant drowns or a drive-by shooting occurs or a natural disaster strikes. Conversely, it is easy to assume that because our lives are going well and nothing dreadful is happening to us, we must be leading guiltless lives.

But according to Jesus, we cannot assess the quantity of another's sin (and subsequent need for repentance) by the quantity of that one's suffering. And for that matter, we cannot assess the quantity of our own righteousness by our lack of suffering. "No," says Jesus, "unless you repent, you will die too!" The strong warning is to stop looking at others in order to evaluate their need for repentance and, instead, to look first at one's own need to repent.

Prayer: *Just and merciful God, it is not always easy for me to see my need to repent. When my life goes smoothly, I assume I am doing all the right things. When I suffer, I wonder what I did to deserve this. Through your Holy Spirit, reveal to me of what I need to repent—and in your mercy, forgive me. In the name of Christ I pray. Amen.*

—K. Cherie Jones
The Upper Room Disciplines 1992

I TURN TO YOU

O Lord God,
    unto whom I turn now in prayer and praise,
    I want to be a stronger person.
    I seek powers equal to my tasks.
I pray to come confidently into your Presence,
    holding up my life for your approval.
I want to bring you my proud accomplishments,
    show you my morning face and my eager heart,
And go forth pleased and satisfied.

But somehow, O Creator,
    it is not usually that way.
I have sought an easy life,
    and I have matched my tasks to my powers.
I must confess that I have preferred
    not to strain the muscles of my spirit
    nor to stretch the sinews of my heart.
I have avoided speaking out for that which is right and just
    because I did not want to be involved in controversy.
I have walked carefully down the middle of the road,
    lest I find some broken human being along the way.
I even have gone to church to give thanks
    that I am not like others—
      lazy, shiftless, improvident, and immoral—
And then I have gone home feeling justified.

I have asked you to use me in your service—
    within limits;
To take my silver and gold—
    sparingly;

To warm my heart and steel my will—
    carefully and with moderation.
You know me, Lord,
    far better than I know myself.
You know I do not want to be unloving,
    but I'm afraid to be loving;
I may be hurt or betrayed.

I do not want to lack faith,
    but I am afraid to trust—
I may be let down.
I do not want to be cowardly,
    but I am afraid to be bold—
I may be labeled as troublesome.
Is that what it means to lead an easy life, O God?
To sidestep any possibility of being hurt,
    to keep aloof from trusting in others,
    to seek shelter from the storm,
        lest the lightning of criticism strike me
        and the thunder of disapproval sound in my ears?
Help me in the spirit of the Lord Jesus Christ
    to pray not for an easy life,
But to be a stronger person.

Let me seek, not tasks equal to my powers,
But powers equal to my tasks.
Let me walk confidently,
    not because of my ability to go in circles,
But because of my steadfast commitment
    to the kind of goals Jesus set.
Let me bring to you, not my proud accomplishments,
But my oftentimes stained,
    occasionally shabby,
    sometimes shining hopes and loves.
Let me come, not just with my morning face and
    eager heart,
But with my tears and aches,

my doubts and fears.
Let me bring to you the whole of my life
    for healing and renewal.
There is so much to be done,
    yet I am not sure I am capable of being a doer.
Keep me from shrugging it all off,
    and keep me from thinking it is all up to me.

Let me pray to be stronger than I am,
    more faithful and loving.
Let me hold steady and remain alive
    to the joy and excitement of being human.
Let me look to you and to others
    as I go out and walk in the footsteps of the Christ,
        in whose name I pray. *Amen.*

—Kenneth G. Phifer
A Book of Uncommon Faith

Day 10

REDEMPTION

*L*ooking back I can't imagine not having made the request to have a happy, normal home life with happy, normal parents. To that request, the NO pervaded my childhood. My unhappy, deeply damaged mother began her journey to alcoholism and death when I was about five years old. It took her over thirty years to kill herself.

The childhood I lived was filled with anxiety, fear, shame, anger, and confusion. The NO answer was clear as I experienced anxiety coming home each day from school for twelve years. The NO drove me into a fetal position in my closet day after day to block out my pain.

College years and afterwards brought some reprieve. My family lived in the Panama Canal Zone and I was, after all, living far away in the United States of America. I "couldn't" often go home. In September 1972, when the word came to me in graduate school that Mother had died, I pulled a hymnbook off the shelf and at midnight, alone in my dormitory room, I sang all four stanzas of "The Strife Is O'er, the Battle Done." Her strife! My strife! Our strife!

Only later, much later, when the wonderful literature about adult children of alcoholics was available— much later when I shared my story and my sorrow with a close friend who was also the adult child of an alcoholic— only then, did the YES begin to blossom in my soul.

Scar tissue replaced the open wounds of my heart. Creative visualization, prayer, and the grace of God have restored a right relationship between my mother and me.

Now, when I see her in my mind's eye, she is young, and lovely, and whole.

From this distance, and in this new place, I am able to look back upon a childhood marred and scarred by negative emotions. From this new place, I see more clearly the myriad of gifts my beloved mother bequeathed to me because of who she was and because of her wounds.

She ran into a bottle to hide from a world which had disappointed and frightened her; a world filled with too much pain. I have chosen to run into the arms of the Lord instead. She gave me the gift of her vulnerability, her tenderness, her compassion. Thank you, Mother, for this gift.

When her body was occupied by that other person who staggered and slurred, and I fled to my room, I had no escape except the inner world of my imagination. There, in my solitude, my intuitive and creative self was born. Thank you, Mother, for this gift.

When her alcoholism transformed my home from a safe space to a place of pain, I felt, lived, and breathed the pain. Sorrow carved into my heart a large capacity for joy and peace which walk hand in hand with redemptive love. Thank you, Mother, for this gift.

Now I am almost the age at which she died. I love and understand and cherish my mother in a holy place in my soul. And, I continue today to honor her for the gifts which she gave to me and to drink deeply from the well of her love for me.

—Carole F. Chase
alive now!

Day 11

WINNERS AND LOSERS

*J*udas Iscariot was one of the twelve apostles whom Jesus chose to be with him in ministry. He was the treasurer of the group—obviously important. For a relatively small sum of money, Judas offered to lead some of the temple guard to the place where Jesus could be taken captive without arousing much of a scene.

We call it Maundy Thursday. And so it was done. Jesus was arrested and led away—the first step toward crucifixion.

What reasons did Judas have for bringing about this betrayal? Much is speculated, little is known. Yet, by early morning, it was clear to Judas that he had sinned by betraying an innocent Jesus. Judas repented, sure of his sin, and returned the money he had been paid. Then Judas, sure of his sin, repentant, yet unable to believe that God loved him, went out and hanged himself.

Peter, also one of the twelve, also chosen to be part of Christ's ministry, was the "rock" of faith upon which Jesus proclaimed his church would be built. Peter was confident, sure that he, perhaps more than any other, would stand with Jesus even unto death. Yet on the same night that Judas led the temple guard to Jesus, Peter would deny three different times that he even knew Jesus. Peter would watch what would befall Jesus from a distance, both physically and spiritually.

After the third denial, the cock crowed, and Peter remembered and realized the implications of what he had done. He went out and wept bitterly. Peter the rock could more accurately be called Peter the "pebble."

Judas and Peter, both spiritually devastated by that long, dark night, both sorrowful for their actions, stood before God. In the face of God's forgiveness, one chose life, and the other chose death. Judas separated himself violently, struck out at his being, sapping from his body the very life, the very promise of the call from God.

Peter accepted God's forgiveness, chose life, and sought the comfort and guidance of the other ten chosen. Peter huddled with them in that upper room, windows shuttered, doors closed, seeking safety and understanding.

Judas shut out God's love and forgiveness—judging himself, punishing himself, not able to hear or feel God's peace even unto his death. Peter, even through his fear, his shock, his shame and guilt, was able to accept God's love and forgiveness, to hear and to feel that call of Jesus, "Peace be with you."

Judas was buried in the potter's field. Peter found new courage, new strength in the forgiveness of God. Peter became the dominant leader in the first generation church. Judas repented of his sin, but refused to accept God's forgiveness.

What about you? Are you capable of closing God out, refusing forgiveness, seeking self-punishment? Unlike what Judas believed, God is never through with us. God seeks us even, perhaps especially, in our weakest times, our darkest hours.

Let go and let God. Let go of self-punishment, and let God's peace heal and forgive.

—Helen R. Neinast and
Thomas C. Ettinger
*What About God? Now
That You're Off to College*

Day 12

OUR ANGER AND GOD'S HEART

*Violence shall no more be heard
in your land,
devastation or destruction
within your borders;*

....

*for the Lord will be your everlasting light,
and your days of mourning shall be ended.*

—Isaiah 60:18, 20

C laim the presence of God's love in whatever way is right for you. Relax your body, and gently breathe each breath as if it were God's breath of life breathed into you. Rest in God. *Remember that you are free to leave this meditation at any point if it becomes too painful or threatening. You are free to change any words or symbols.*

When you feel ready, ask Christ, the Healer, to guide you to some hurtful memory. If this is the first time you have experienced memory-healing prayer, you may wish to begin with a memory that is not too traumatic. Ask the Healer to go ahead of you into that place where the event occurred. The place itself, the very space, will need healing. Sense, or inwardly picture, how the Healer fills that space with warmth and light. Enter the space of the memory when it feels safe for you. Sit quietly with the Healer, or walk around, seeing the warm streams of light flowing into every part of the room, across the floor, ceiling, windows, furniture, doors. Breathe the new air of the space until you begin to feel peaceful and reassured there. This may be enough for this time. You can always come back later.

When you feel ready, ask the Healer to invite in the other person who was involved in your hurt. Picture or sense the other entering as the child.

How do you feel as the other person enters? Listen to your body as well as to your feelings. You are safe. Christ, the Healer, is there enfolding you and protecting you. But you are free to leave at any point. God's love does not force us to enter or to remain in places of pain.

Now let yourself feel fully. Do you feel anger, bitterness, rage, grief? If so, do not contrive reconciliation. Your anger is there for a reason. Does your anger or grief feel focused somewhere in your body? In your heart? In your abdomen? In your face or hands? Behind your eyes? You may wish to lay a comforting hand upon your body, or think of the Healer gently touching you.

Let your feelings take a symbolic form: a bird, or an animal, or a color, or storm clouds, or torrential rivers, or anything else that is spontaneous for you. Let these feelings and their power flow directly into the heart of the Healer who stands there between you and the other person. Let them flow into the Healer's body as long and as forcefully as you feel the need. Let yourself express what you feel with words or images or tears. You may even want to draw what you feel.

This may be enough for one time. Perhaps later (maybe much later) you may be ready to let the child within the other person express also what he or she feels; to share her or his own woundedness, grief, anger, or fear. If it is still too soon for this, it is enough just to be willing to be in the same space with the other person of your memory, held by God, letting your feelings go directly into the heart of Christ.

As you move back to the present time and place, let the entrance to that door of the past remain open, so that its healing light will shine along your path of return. If you decide to go back to that place of memory at some later time, the healing will move to an even deeper place within you.

When you think of that other person, try to see the hurting child within him or her, also held by God's tenderness. This is a powerful and effective way to pray for our "enemy." We do not at any time have to force love or even liking within ourselves. Neither do we have to force the feelings of full forgiveness. It is enough to see the other person as also God's beloved child, held by God. Later, the feelings of forgiveness will come spontaneously.

Rest quietly again in God's presence, gently massaging your face, hands, and arms, becoming aware of the chair, the floor beneath you. When ready, open your eyes and conclude your meditation.

—Flora Slosson Wuellner
Heart of Healing, Heart of Light

BUT COULD I DO IT 489 MORE TIMES?

I squirmed in my seat and wished Sunday school was over. Mostly the class is okay. It was just that the day was bright and warm and I wanted to be out riding my new trail bike. Instead, I was listening to the teacher talk about forgiveness. She said, "Peter asked Jesus if he should forgive someone as many as seven times. But how many times did Jesus tell him we should forgive?"

A girl shot her hand in the air. "Jesus told Peter we're supposed to forgive seventy *times* seven," she said.

I picked up my pencil and multiplied 70 x 7. It came to *four hundred ninety!* "Wow!" I said to myself, "Jesus sure is big on forgiveness." Little did I know that I was soon to find out how hard it is to forgive even once.

The minute I got home from Sunday school, I called my best friend, Jeff. He brought his old bike over and asked if he could try out my new one while I changed clothes. "Sure," I told him. "But don't be gone long."

A half hour later I was standing out in the street, looking first one direction and then the other. Jeff hadn't come back, and I was getting madder by the second. When I finally saw him turn the corner, he was pushing my bike instead of riding it. "What happened?" I hollered as I raced toward him.

"I had an accident," he mumbled. I looked down at his torn jeans and scraped knee. But what really got my attention was the scratch on my bike and the bent pedal.

"*My new bike!*" I almost choked on the words. "Look what you did to it."

"I know, Scott," he said, "I'm sorry."

"So you're *sorry*," I said, spitting the words out. "Sorry isn't going to cover up the scratch or fix the pedal. What were you doing anyway?

"A guy asked me if I wanted to race," he started to explain. "There was some loose gravel in the street and I…"

Jeff's words trailed off. It didn't matter that he hadn't finished. I got the picture. "It's just as well you don't have a brain," I yelled at him, hating the tears that stung my eyes. "Because if you did you wouldn't know what to do with it anyway."

"It was an accident," Jeff shouted back. "So why don't you just cool off?" He grabbed his own bike and started wheeling it down the street. I noticed he was limping. "I bet he's faking," I thought bitterly. Right then I knew that if I never saw Jeff Barton again it would be too soon.

That night I told my dad what happened. He was able to fix the pedal. "But there's nothing we can do about the scratch," he said. "After awhile, there will be other scratches, and you'll forget about this one."

"No I won't," I said to myself. "Every time I look at it I'll think about Jeff and remember that he's my *ex*-friend."

Jeff and I had been friends for a long time. If he wasn't at my house, I was at his. Not being together was hard to get used to. A couple of times I started to call him, but when I remembered what he did, I hung up the phone. Whenever I thought about the fun we used to have together, loneliness gathered inside me like a gray cloud. But then I would remember why we weren't friends anymore and get mad all over again. Jeff had damaged my bike. If anyone was going to make the first call, he should be the one to do it.

The next Saturday I was feeling especially bored and asked my dad to play catch with me. "I can't today, Scott," he said. "I'm playing tennis. Why don't you call Jeff?"

"After what he did to my bike, he's no friend of mine," I said. My dad slid a glance at me like he was thinking something, then decided not to say it. I watched him get his tennis racquet out of the closet. "Who you playing with?" I asked.

"Tom Sampson. I called him this morning."

"You called Tom Sampson?" I couldn't believe I'd heard him right. "Is he the same man you got so mad at over a business deal?

My dad nodded. "The same one."

"I thought you said you weren't going to have anything to do with him any more." I felt disappointed that my dad had gone back on his word. "And now you called him to play tennis?"

"That's right," my dad said. "We had been friends for a long time—too long to let one disagreement come between us. One of us had to make the first move, and I decided it would be me."

I watched from the window as my dad got in the car and drove away. I wondered what it would be like getting back together with someone after you had had a fight with them. Very awkward, I decided. You wouldn't know what to say and neither would the other guy. Probably you'd just stand around looking at each other. "It's better to be alone than go through that," I thought. I flipped on the TV. There was nothing worth watching, so I turned it off. I picked up a book but couldn't concentrate. Jeff's number kept going round and round in my head. Before I could think of all the reasons why I shouldn't call, I dialed. Jeff answered the phone. I swallowed hard before I said, "Hi, this is Scott."

"Well . . . hi," Jeff stammered like I had really taken him by surprise.

I paused, not sure what to say next. "You doing anything?"

"Huh-uh," he answered.

"How about playing a little catch?"

Jeff hesitated for a second or so, but it seemed like an hour. "Well, why not?" he said. "Where should I meet you?"

"How about at the park in five minutes?"

I put the receiver down and took a deep breath. My dad was right: if you want to be friends again, someone has to make the first move. What he hadn't told me was how good you feel after you do it.

I got on my bike and I headed toward the park. While I pedaled down the street, I remembered the Sunday school class when we talked about forgiving seventy times seven. "It was plenty hard forgiving just once," I muttered to myself. "I don't know about doing it four hundred eighty-nine *more* times!"

—Mary Montgomery
Pockets

FORGIVENESS

*F*orgiveness is giving up the right to retaliate. Forgiveness is the willingness to have something happen the way it happened. It's not true that you can't forgive something; it's a matter of the will, and you always have the choice. Forgiveness is never dependent on what the other person does or does not do; it is always under our control. Forgiveness is giving up the insistence on being understood. St. Paul said, "[Love] seeketh not her own" (2 Cor. 13:5, KJV). Jesus forgave those who crucified him. This is a radically new way of thinking. For those who accept and practice this discipline, there is a release of energy and a sense of freedom.

—Pixie Koestline Hammond
For Everything There Is a Season

NO STONE

No stone
in Jesus'
rugged hand.
Instead he wrote
imperishably
in the sand.

—Thomas John Carlisle
alive now!

Week Three

Here Is Joy, Here Is Hope

O come, let us sing to the Lord;
  let us make a joyful noise to the rock of our salvation!
Let us come into his presence with thanksgiving;
  let us make a joyful noise to him with songs of praise!
                                          Psalm 95:1-2

We boast in our hope of sharing the glory of God. And not
only that, but we also boast in our sufferings, knowing that
suffering produces endurance, and endurance produces
character, and character produces hope, and hope does not
disappoint us, because God's love has been poured into our
hearts through the Holy Spirit.
                                          Romans 5:2-5

CELEBRATION BEYOND TEARS

And he took a cup, and when he had given thanks he said,
"Take this, and divide it among yourselves . . . "

—Luke 22:17

*O*ne of the never-failing topics
of interest, curiosity, and comparison
on an island, which is seldom even mentioned
in the city or the suburb,
is that of wells and water supply:
whether yours is dug or drilled,
how deep you had to go,
how many gallons you can pump per minute,
their flavor, color, odor, dependability of supply.
The possibilities for fascinating debate
seem almost endless.

Which is not all that surprising, really,
since without that clear and flowing liquid
life cannot continue. We may survive
for several weeks without the staff of life—
the loaf; whereas without the cup
we perish within hours.

When Jesus lifted up the cup
(and it is interesting to note how Luke
sets cup before the loaf, reversing Matthew,
Mark, and the tradition of the church),
he lifted up the liquid symbol of our life
in its precarious dependence.
The following day, his desperate cry,

"I thirst," from high upon the cross
lives out the pouring, giving, sharing
sacrifice portrayed within this gesture.

Yet in giving us the cup
He gave us more than mere survival,
far more than prison fare of bread and water;
the wine within that cup still speaks
of passion and of joy,
the full and free commitment
known in covenant, high ceremony,
marriage, consecration, coronation,
the offering of life in love and service,
the pledging of oneself to another,
to a cause, to a kingdom, to a promise
that is someday to be won.

And there was joy there,
yes, despite the horror soon to be,
despite the presence in that cup,
around that hallowed table,
of pain and bitterness so sharp
that he would ask, that very night,
the cup be taken from him.
For wine brings us to laughter,
making faces to shine, eyes sparkle,
lips to form in joyous song.
So in the cup he pours us
celebration beyond tears,
reconciliation beyond all sad betrayal,
and a vision and a hope so sure
it can brighten every shadowed place
with the radiance of eternal dawn.

So in this final living parable,
Christ leaves us as his last bequest,
life beyond death,

bright joy beyond all grief,
trust beyond reasonable doubt,
and his own self, both host and feast,
presiding at God's universal table
to welcome the whole family of being.

So welcome me this night, Lord Christ;
hold to my lips the cup of your rich love
and true salvation, and hear my pledge
to love and serve you all my days.
Amen.

—J. Barrie Shepherd
Seeing with the Soul

Day 16

A LITTLE MADNESS

*W*e have been talking about joy; akin to joy is hope, and hope gives us the energy for our Christian Walk.

Zorba is one of my favorite movie and stage productions. The theater experience was especially memorable for me when Anthony Quinn played Zorba. The climax of the drama is two men—Zorba and his boss—dancing. The boss's money is invested in an untried invention to bring timber down a mountain. The wood is badly needed by the community, and it is to be used to reinforce the walls of an old mine which, it is hoped, will restore economic life to the village. Everyone turned out to watch the great occasion. Anticipation turned quickly to gloom as the weight of the logs caused the unproven slide to collapse. The dejected man, whose money was lost, pondered leaving the village. But the words of Zorba get his attention: "I like you too much not to say it, you've got everything, except one thing—madness. A man needs a little madness or else . . . he never dares cut the rope and be free."

Then standing before the dismal pile of rubble, Zorba begins to laugh, and says, "Hey Boss, did you ever see a more splendiferous crash?"

With renewed perspective, the boss asks, "Teach me to dance, will you?" The story closes with the two dancing and celebrating life at the sight of their greatest failure.

At the heart of the Christian faith is Easter, and Easter is about the little madness to be free to dance and celebrate because there has been a resurrection. The stupendous crash that took place on Golgotha, the huge stone shouting no to life as it was placed over the cave tomb in which Jesus' body was laid—that crash is swallowed up in laughing and alleluias and shouting and dancing.

Peter summarized the meaning of our Easter faith: "Blessed be the God and Father of our Lord Jesus Christ! By his great mercy we have been born anew to a living hope through the resurrection of Jesus Christ from the dead."

Each of the Gospels tells the Easter story slightly differently. But in each telling, there is the suggestion of more than just a little madness of hope. Luke tells of the women going to the tomb early on Sunday morning, taking spices to anoint Jesus' body. But when they go into the tomb, they cannot find the body. Two men in dazzling apparel frighten them as one of them says, "Why do you seek the living among the dead?" Then he reminds them of how Jesus Christ had told them that he would be delivered into the hands of sinful men and be crucified and, on the third day, rise. It is then that they remember, and they return to the eleven disciples to share the great good news.

The result: "But these words seemed to them an idle tale, and they did not believe them" (Luke 24:11). A little madness there.

In each of the Gospels it's the same. In Mark's Gospel, the women who see Jesus on Easter morning "said nothing to anyone, for they were afraid." A little madness. In Matthew's Gospel, the authorities tell the guards they must "tell people his disciples came by night and stole him away while we were asleep." A little madness. In John's Gospel, the disciples lock themselves in a room, in fear and despair. A little madness.

But the madness changes. Something is added when the fact of the resurrection dawns fully upon them. Hope is added, and with it, the little madness of hope.

—Maxie Dunnam
The Workbook on the Christian Walk

THE STORY OF ANNA WHITE

*L*ast Good Friday morning I drove to a nearby state institution for mentally-handicapped adults to help the chaplain conduct a worship service. About fifty of the residents arrived for the service, walking into the chapel noisily, arranging themselves haphazardly in the wooden pews. Moving silently among them was Anna White.

She was slender as a reed, dark-skinned with white hair pulled tightly into a bun, at least eighty years old. Her dark, quick eyes watched every movement of the service: the opening of the book of scripture, the veneration of the cross, the sitting and standing of the congregation. But to the prayers and hymns, she made no response. Anna White was deaf.

After the service, as her companions pushed past her to leave the chapel, I motioned for her to come up to the front. Taking her silently by the hand, I led her to the heavy crucifix hanging high on the sanctuary wall. Reaching up, I touched the hands of the figure of Jesus. Then I touched my own palms, first one, then the other, making the sign language gesture for the name of Jesus.

Anna White understood. Quickly she touched her own palms, making the Jesus sign. Then, her lean body swaying gracefully from side to side, Anna White danced down the empty aisle, holding her hands aloft and making the sign for Jesus over and over in silent rhythm. Up and down the aisle she danced, then out into the bleak landscape of the institution, still signing Jesus with her whole being.

That Good Friday morning, Anna White danced the cross, herself a sign of resurrection life.

—Marilyn Wickel
alive now!

CHRIST COMES RUNNING

Christ comes running,
eyes bright with joy,
and shatters the ice inside me
with laughter and a hug.

"But I'm not worthy"
does not cut it with such a deity.
Who am I to dampen his party
with my fumbling for humble words?

Holy parties don't happen
on my command—
only on my account—
when this lavish Lord
sees an inch of growth in me.

—Jim Frisbie
alive now!

PREPARE TO CELEBRATE!

Psalm 148
"Let them all praise the name of the Lord!"

Introduction: Psalm 148 is a hymn of creation, inviting both heaven and earth to sing praise. Part I calls upon the heavenly creation (verses 1-2) and heavenly phenomena (verses 3-4). Then follows a refrain (verses 5-6) sung by the Temple choir. Part II is addressed to the earthly creation made of "the deep" and things that arise from it (verses 7-8), the earth and things on it (verses 9-10), and the people on the earth (verses 11-12). A second refrain follows in verses 13-14a.

Preparation: No somber moods today! This psalm is a hymn of unrestrained joy. Prepare to celebrate!

Read Psalm 148: Read the psalm the first time, noting the different orders of creation. Then after a brief silence, go back and "sing" it as the great hymn of praise it is.

Reflection: Compare the biblical text of the psalm with the great hymn, "Praise the Lord! Ye Heavens Adore Him." Compare this psalm with Psalm 104. Which do you prefer?

Prayer: Let your prayer be your own hymn of praise to the God of creation. Add those created things for which you are most thankful.

—Donald E. Collins
Like Trees That Grow Beside a Stream

Day 20

THE STATIONS OF THE CROSS

*T*here is much in our human nature that resists living the contradictions; much in us that tries to avoid tension, avoid life torn between the poles, avoid living on the cross. Though I abhor war, I continue to pay war taxes; I resist life on that particular cross. But in that failure, I am caught in yet another tension, impaled on yet another cross, torn between my own convictions and my inability to act them out.

I have come to believe that our resistance to such crosses, our resistance to God's will, is itself an aspect of the cruciform nature of reality. If we can recognize it as such, then our resistance, our tendency to contradict God, will generate great energy for life. By living fully in those tensions, neither denying nor ignoring them, we will be pulled open to the power of the Spirit.

I see this power illustrated in scripture, and especially in the Old Testament. The Old Testament is full of people resisting God: trying to trick God, to outwit God, to fly in the face of God's commands, to outdo God in the haggling of the marketplace. I like that because it humanizes the spiritual life. It assumes that God is a person who can be dragged into the human struggle. How often in our secular piety we treat God as an abstract principle who cannot enter the realities of the flesh! In doing so we deprive ourselves of a great source of energy for life—I mean a God who contends with us, as the angel wrestled with Jacob.

I believe it is God's will that I devote my whole self to the establishment of peace on earth. But how I struggle against that will! How I try to bargain with God, arguing that other claims on my life must be honored too: the claims of family, or career, of limited time and energy, of my prudent fears about the consequences of responding too fully to what the Lord requires. But as I live in that resistance, as I acknowledge it and confess it to myself and others, slowly my life is pulled open. As I live in the tension created by my fear of confronting war taxes, slowly my life is pulled open to other ways in which I can witness for peace. I look within my family and find ways of living in harmony. I look at my career and find ways of using my gifts toward the creation of a peaceable kingdom. My very resistance, my contention with God, stretches me to discover what I *can* do to witness to the light. This is one reason to attend to our resistance, to stay with it until it opens us to something new.

There is another reason to trust our resistance to the cross, for some crosses are false, not given by God, but placed upon us by a heedless world and received by an unhealthy part of ourselves. Christian tradition has too many examples of masochism masquerading as the way of the cross. And the church is full of people who submit all too easily to injustices which ought to be fought. So we have the problem of distinguishing valid crosses from invalid ones, crosses which lead toward the centerpoint from crosses which lead to desolation. I do not know of any abstract principles by which the one can be told from the other. Perhaps our natural resistance is as good a test as any. Resist any cross that comes your way. Boldly become a pole of opposition; live the contradiction. The false crosses will fall away, while those we must accept will stay there in the middle of our lives, pulling right and left, up and down, until they pull us open at our true center, a center where we are one with God, a center which we find only on the way of the cross.

—Parker J. Palmer
Weavings

RUNNING TO GOD

Read Psalm 16.

Preserve me, O God, for in thee I take refuge.
—Psalm 16:1 (RSV)

One of my favorite hideouts as a child was an old hackberry tree in our backyard. It was at various times a gigantic airplane that I piloted through the clouds, a tall-masted sailing ship which rocked rhythmically in the summer wind, and a secret retreat to which I scurried when the grass needed mowing on a Saturday morning. It was a safe place of refuge—a familiar, friendly, safe place where I could forget about the world and be drawn into great dreams and adventures.

As I grew up I learned just how much God is like that special place of refuge. In God we have a special place to retreat when problems and pressures build up. But there is a big difference between that childhood experience and my adult relationship with God. The hackberry tree provided a place of forgetting, of childish avoidance. Now, though, I run not away from life but to God, because in God I find refreshing power. My time with God renews me so that I can face scary times with courage.

Taking refuge is not weakness. Indeed, in our refuge we find strength and renewal.

PRAYER: Dear Lord, in faith I seek refuge in You so that Your power and purpose can flow through me. Amen.

THOUGHT FOR THE DAY
God is a storehouse of strength and hope for this day.

Roger Pierce (Virginia)
The Upper Room

Week Four

Turning Toward God

Return to the Lord, your God,
  for he is gracious and merciful,
slow to anger, and abounding in steadfast love,
  and relents from punishing.

Joel 2:13

[Jesus said] "Very truly, I tell you, no one can see the kingdom of God without being born from above."

John 3:3

JOURNEY WITHOUT END

I grew up thinking that I could and would attain perfection if only I tried hard enough and was very good. (In fact, I had lived a perfect life until I went to college!)

But I discovered that I was not perfect and never would be.

The journey toward perfection was a stark road, full of "don'ts" and "shoulds" . . . full of hairshirts and punishment.

Now that I am grown, I read about things like singleness of purpose and purity of heart. My tendency is to place these virtues in the same category as perfection—unattainable fantasies.

But in some special moments I feel a sense of the Holy One, a sense of the divine presence, and I have a glimpse of what it means to walk with God on the path of holiness.

When I am quiet enough inside to notice a sunset, to hear the early-morning sounds, to know when a friend needs someone to listen, I am for a moment participating in God's journey. I think that this is singleness of purpose—being with God on God's journey.

The journey of holiness is not a journey with a beginning or an end. It is a path which winds alongside our own roads. And when we are in tune with God and ourselves, we sometimes find ourselves on that path. It is a rich, beautiful road of oneness with God.

—Beth A. Richardson
alive now!

Day 23

SHADOWBOUND

O nce upon a time there was a man who lived in the middle of a desert. Yet, that was not quite true. It would be better to say that he was a prisoner of the desert. You see, somehow and sometime in the past our friend had acquired the habit of following his shadow, and only his shadow. It was a relentless and unbending compass which he obeyed completely and followed without question. Every morning when the sun came up he began walking in the direction his shadow pointed. As the sun traced its slow crescent across the sky he followed the subtle bending of his shadow. By the end of the day he had traced a rough oval and was nearly back to where he had started in the morning. While his course varied a little with the seasons of the year and the speed he walked, it wasn't much, and it was never enough to allow him to leave the desert.

This had been going on for as long as he could remember. It was familiar and comfortable, the only way he knew. Yet he also had to admit that it often left him feeling trapped and alone. Sometimes he wondered what it would be like to face the sun instead of always turning his back to it and walking the other way. And he longed to see if there might not be something more to the world than the desert, but he never seemed to have enough resolve ever to do anything different.

Then one morning, while it was still dark, as he was preparing to set out again, something came and spoke to him. It was a voice. At least it was more like a voice than anything else. It said, "JUST STOP IT." That's all, "JUST STOP IT."

JUST STOP IT? He didn't know how he knew, but he knew without a doubt that what was meant by this was following his shadow. Just stop it. Could it be that simple? What a lovely thought. Yet it was a foreboding thought as well. Certainly there was joy and hope in what the voice suggested, but there was also fear and dread because following his shadow was the only way he knew to get around—such as it was!

About this time the sun came up, and with it the powerful tug of his growing shadow. He tried to resist it but could not. Yet all that day, even as he obediently followed his shadow, the memory of the Voice and the experience of the morning stayed with him. It stayed with him through the night, too. And while he made no significant changes over the next few days, it was enough just to have some hope.

Then one morning, just a moment before dawn, he suddenly turned his back to the dark, western horizon and faced the glow in the east. It was done almost before he realized what he was doing. The freedom to do it happened in a moment. And he recognized in his new freedom the presence again of the Voice, which lovingly offered him what he could not offer himself.

The rising sun in front of him was brighter and more wonderful than he had imagined anything could ever be. As the sun cut across the sky that first day it was all he could do just to stand there and face the light, turning slowly now to keep his shadow in back of him! There was no question about going anywhere. Yet, as the day passed, his shadow became less and less intimidating and his new freedom more and more familiar, even if it was just to stand still.

Finally, one morning, the Voice came again. As with the other times, he could not fully describe what happened, only that the Voice brought him another gift. The gift this time was a sense of direction.

Slowly, he put one foot in front of the other, fixed his gaze on some distant mountains, and set out. He wasn't sure where he was going, but at least he wasn't still going around in circles. And he certainly didn't feel alone anymore.

—David M. Griebner
Weavings

STANDING IN GOD'S PRESENCE

*R*ead Psalm 139:1-6.

We can celebrate the occasions when we have glimpses into God's power and glory that surround us, but the reverse side of that is that God is continually aware of us. The psalmist is astonished at such knowledge. Nor is God an observer of our lives from the outside: God is intimately aware of our thoughts before we utter them, of our hidden motives, of our most secret emotions. God knows us better than we know ourselves. We cannot fool God even though we can fool ourselves.

It is one thing to hold a theoretical view of the power of God. Then it can be talked about and debated. The psalmist is not giving a lecture on the attributes of God, however. It is quite a different thing to experience the searching knowledge of God, to know that we stand in the presence of One who cannot be fooled, to whom no lie can be told, no excuse given, One who rips away from us every feeble attempt to cover up our fears, our sins, our hopes and dreams. The psalmist speaks from such an experience of God's knowledge.

Knowing that we stand in the presence of such a God is both frightening and comforting. It is frightening because there is much we would hide. It is comforting because ultimately there is One who know us thoroughly, who understands us even more than we can understand ourselves, and who still claims us as children of God.

Prayer: *Your knowledge, O God, is too great for us to comprehend, yet we know that in that knowledge is our hope for redemption. Let us not be afraid of being known by you. Amen.*

—Catherine Gunsalus González
Disciplines 1992

THE CRUX

Crux: Latin for cross;
now means the point of decision.
[Didn't it always?]
Also appearing in words like
　crucify,
　　crucifer,
　　　crucible,
excruciating.

He wants me to take up one of *those*?
And follow him *there*?

Crucial decision.

—Lois Duffield
alive now!

DO I HAVE TO TAKE HIM WITH ME?

"Oh, Mom, does Bill have to go with me to Sunday school, too?"

I groaned. I was ten years old and had always been an only child. Suddenly, this stranger named Bill had come to live with us.

He was different; "slow to learn" Mom had said before she brought him home. She had talked about how I should share my room and my toys with him since he had been taken away from his own home because of abuse and neglect.

Bill was only six months older than I, but everything he did seemed wrong to me. He didn't like to take showers, he left my toys in all the wrong places, and he followed me around like a shadow.

Although I was sorry to hear about how Bill had been mistreated, I really didn't like having a foster brother—and one who was slow to learn at that.

"Richard," Mom continued, "Bill may be with us for some time, and he hasn't been in Sunday school for several years. I would like him to go with you to your class next Sunday."

"But he might embarrass me in front of my friends, Mom," I replied. "Why can't he go with you to your class, anyway?"

Of course, I knew I would lose this argument. Mom always was wise and sensible. She usually had the final word around our house.

On Sunday morning, I told Bill to go into class first. I didn't want him to sit next to me, so I waited outside the door until everyone else went in. Then I sat on the far side of the circle.

Bill wasn't sitting near anyone. He sat by himself.

"Good morning, everyone, " said our teacher, Mr. Stephens. "We have a visitor today. Did someone bring him?"

I froze and didn't say a word. Then, as I thought he would, Bill said hello and gave his name. His speech was slurred. Then he pointed to me, and I just hung my head, wondering what my friends were thinking. Some of them began to snicker and laugh.

"Did you bring him, Richard?"

"Yes, sir," I meekly replied.

"We're always glad to have visitors," Mr. Stephens commented. "Bill, would you like to read the first part of the lesson today?" he asked.

"Oh, no," I thought. Bill can't read well, and everyone will laugh at him. I began to feel angry at Mom and Mr. Stephens both. How could they do this to me?

With difficult speech, Bill began telling his own Bible story from the Old Testament, even though our lesson was about Jesus and the disciples. I felt like hiding under my chair.

When Bill finished, everyone looked at me and then at Mr. Stephens. I couldn't look directly into anyone's eyes. Finally, Mr. Stephens said, "Bill, thank you for sharing that story. It's special to me, too. I hope all of you have your own special Bible verses and stories you have memorized."

Then he said something about our class being a place where everyone felt welcome and accepted. I began to feel a little guilty. After all, Bill was with a group of strangers, and these were all my friends.

I looked at Bill and felt surprised that he could remember a Bible story he must have learned years ago. Mom had said that Bill hadn't been to Sunday school in a long time. Yet he retold a story that even I didn't know well.

It's hard to explain, but I began thinking more about Bill and less about me. I got up and moved to the other side of the circle and sat next to Bill.

"Mr. Stephens," I explained, "Bill has come to live with us for a while. He doesn't read too well, but I'll help him with the words in our lesson if that's okay."

"That's what being a friend is all about. Please begin, Richard—and Bill."

—Richard Whitaker
Pockets

Day 26

INTUITION OF WHOLENESS

Our lives are stretched between two great poles. The one, planted in the soil of hope, marks the fulfillment of our every desire for transformation, whether in great things or small. Astir in each of us is an intuition of wholeness and beauty, a glimpse of all the shattered or misshapen pieces of our life lovingly gathered into the form of our best and truest self. Each of us has known holy moments showing us a time when we could look outward upon the world without fear and gaze inward upon ourselves without shame. Deep within the energies that bear us lifeward is a conviction that we are not closed systems, not frozen pillars of possibility like Lot's wife. The first pole bears a banner emblazoned with Paul's bold prophecy: "Lo! I tell you a mystery . . . we shall all be changed" (1 Cor. 15:51, RSV).

The other pole, driven into the earth of experience, stakes out the reign of our fear of change, our resistance to the new, our grip upon the familiar and the comfortable. Human beings, alone among creatures, are not born into a genetically predetermined world. Among our life tasks is the construction of a world in which we can dwell. Each of us, snail-like, bears a home-world upon our back, its weight both burden and comfort through our days. Its recesses shelter living memories of our past; its contours shape our expectations for the future. The prospect of change challenges our "world," insisting that something of our life's labor must be undone. Will the gain outsize the loss? Engraved upon the second pole is Augustine's response to God's persistent wooing: "Let me wait a little longer."

The spiritual life embraces these two great poles of human longing. The outlines of the final transformation for which we hope are already being etched through our daily struggles with faithfulness. And these daily struggles remind us that, like Gulliver in the land of the Lilliputians, our capacity to effect our own transformation is bound fast by a thousand gossamer attachments to personal as well as collective "worlds." We do not engage these struggles unaided, however. The Spirit takes our part, nudging us toward greater liberty. "Where the Spirit of the Lord is, there is freedom. And we all, with unveiled face, beholding the glory of the Lord, are being changed into his likeness from one degree of glory to another . . ."(2 Cor. 3:17-18, RSV). Here is the drama of Lent and Easter writ large across our lives. Stripped of illusions of self-improvement, we begin to perceive the true glory of the crucified Lord. More remarkably, in perceiving this glory we are also receiving its steady impress upon our life, conforming us to the image of Christ. In this conformation resides the font of freedom.

—John S. Mogabgab
Weavings

Day 27

SAYING GOODBYES

*I*ntegral to life are our hellos and goodbyes. We have to say goodbye to the old in order to say hello to the new. Healthy people can say their goodbyes and move on; unhealthy people put it off and even work hard to deny their goodbyes.

Mary Magdalene had to learn to say goodbye to the Jesus she loved in this life so she could say hello to a new dimension of his presence. She could *not* hold on to the Jesus of history. Only when she could say goodbye could she move on in her faith story.

At any age people say goodbyes. But as we grow older, it seems we have to say a lot of goodbyes. We say goodbye to a friend who moves to another city to live with a son, or goodbye to a dear friend who has died. If we are ill for a time, we say goodbye to some independence. It is natural to experience some grief over each of these.

But we can find ways to turn these losses into gains. The "goodbyes" of old age can become the "hellos" of a new life. We can learn to be centered on God's work in our lives. We can gain perspective and a deeper insight into the true meaning of everything. The psalmist called it "a heart of wisdom" (Psalm 90:12, RSV). So, "Goodbye and hello!"

PRAYER————————————————————————————

Loving God, it is hard to say goodbye to what and whom we love; we do get attached to people and things in this life. But give us your grace to let go of what we need to let go of so that we may grow in your love. *Amen.*

—Richard L. Morgan
No Wrinkles on the Soul

DAILY DANCING WITH THE HOLY ONE

*F*or years I waited for God to do big things in my life. When I was fourteen, I was confirmed on Palm Sunday. A few days later I would go to Communion for the first time. I expected something big to happen. I would feel different, be different. I would know that God was real in a way I had never known before. Communion was Maundy Thursday night. I remember the quiet, the darkened sanctuary, the rustle of our crisp white robes, the papery wafer, my first taste of wine—strange and bitter but warming. I waited. Nothing happened, or so I thought.

I desired so deeply to know God, to experience the presence of God as I communed that first time. I wanted an experience like Paul being cast down on the road—something immense, undeniable. Slowly I am learning that in life the ways of God are more often gentle and quiet than earthshaking. What I did not realize as a teenager was that those subtle perceptions—the rustling robes, the first taste of wine—could be turning points. As it does for a ballerina pirouetting on toe, a turning point allows us to dance in new directions, to encounter all of life more fully. A living faith embraces both movement and stillness, the dynamic tension that creates dance. We may not always know the next steps, but in every moment we are invited to listen and learn.

Years ago when I started to dance, I was bewildered to learn that I could not keep my balance by holding my arms out—my common response for holding others at a distance and keeping things in control. I could only keep my balance by keeping my "center," which is located in the solar plexus, my very gut. Only with my center could I get close, risk, be momentarily off-balance, leap and turn, and (usually) not fall.

Every day I am challenged to keep my center, to keep God as my balance point. Often that seems easier when it comes to the "big" things in life because somehow I have the idea that God is supposed to be there. God is big, I learned as a child. Therefore God will be in "big" things. But for the most part all things, big and small, are composed of the seemingly mundane moments of daily life. And it is these little moments that often become turning points of faith—moments that move me, draw me, call me, push me toward a life that is lived out of love, not fear; moments that invite me to choose life over death, blessing over curse.

Each moment is the occasion for a potential conversion that calls us to our very center, to be the people we most fully, deeply, authentically are. Conversion reveals the heart of God that lies deep within each of us. It challenges us to take off our masks, take down our defenses, to be open, vulnerable in order that we might fully receive and freely give. In each moment, God invites us to enter the dance of life, to dance who we are, what we do, and who we are in relation to others and all of creation, to dance every step with God as our center. . . .

Is God really present in the mundane moments of life? What do such moments have to do with who I am called to be as a child of God? At times God moves grandly, boldly in my life, and I shiver with excitement and confidence—or am overwhelmed with awe. But those times are the exceptions rather than the rule. I am most challenged to be confident of my faith when my back aches from sitting at the computer too long, my eyes blur from staring at the screen, a deadline is imminent, and all I really want to do is sleep because there was a fire one street over last night and the fire department kept the neighborhood awake half the night. Can even this be a turning point, a *learning* point? . . .

When I crawl into bed at night, I reflect on my day and ask to see those moments that I may have overlooked, those places where God was moving. Where did God touch me, heal me, challenge me? What were the hard points, the turning points of the day? Where was God in them? What gave me life today? In this abbreviated version of what in classical Christian tradition has been called "examen of conscience" (or consciousness examen), I do not always like what I see. At other times I am surprised or excited. But in either case, I am stuck if I am not willing to move, to turn—either back from that which draws me away from God or toward that which draws me closer to God.

Now, instead of waiting for God to do big things in my life, I seek to dance in the embrace of the Holy One by fully encountering each marvelous, mundane moment. The little moments of life can draw us closer to God. If the momentary is not sacred, neither is the momentous. If each moment is sacred—a time and place where we encounter God—life itself is sacred.

We must keep dancing, keep turning. We must turn to the corners of our lives, look behind trees and trucks and trapdoors, leap over mountains and peer into molehills—for there is the stuff, the mighty simple stuff of conversion. By opening ourselves to the sacred moments of ordinary time, we pray without ceasing, we seek and find. Our eyes are opened, our ears unstopped, our tongues loosed, our hands freed, and our legs unshackled. The lame do indeed leap for joy. We turn with moments of grace that move us into life, but the center remains the same—God.

—Jean M. Blomquist
Weavings

Week Five

Love Beyond Understanding

O give thanks to the Lord, for he is good;
  his steadfast love endures forever!
                                    Psalm 118:1

For God so loved the world that he gave his only Son, so
that everyone who believes in him may not perish but may
have eternal life.
                                    John 3:16

This is my commandment, that you love one another as I
have loved you.
                                    John 15:12

GOD'S COVENANT LOVE

Read Romans 8:1-9.

In Christ Jesus the life-giving law of the Spirit has set you free from the law of sin and death. —Romans 8:2 (NEB)

I first began to recognize the gentle persistence of God's covenant love while working as a therapist in an Oklahoma hospital. There I met an extraordinary couple. Though the wife was dying, there existed between her and her husband a love that not many are gifted to experience. They truly loved each other into being. I used to hurry to get to this patient's room early in the hope of spending time with them, to see them being in love after so many years.

I soon became confused as to who was ministering to whom. I felt this woman reaching out to me. As her condition worsened and she was no longer able to speak, our conversations became a process of unspoken discernment. And it was in the silence of her soul in that room that she called my soul forth—a process which amazed me. I, a very chatty person, experienced transforming love in the silence. And it is a continued source of amazement to me that this woman so near death should take the time to love one more person as she beheld the hand of God.

PRAYER: God, author of all love, help us to show Your love in whatever our circumstances. We know not Your ways, but Your love endures even through death. Amen.

Love is eternal, and God's covenant extends to all generations.

—Linda M. Small (Illinois)
The Upper Room

I Am Not Sure of Love

O Lord, I live in a world of angry men and women.
I am often angry myself at threats to my values,
at brutal disregard for the institutions I hold
dear.
Where do I belong in such a world?
Where does the Lord Jesus belong?
Is love weak,
  too weak to be creative?
Is compassion sheer sentiment?
Is this a time to be hard and tough?
My emotions tell me so some of the time.
Then at other times I see him moving
   amid the shadows of history.
I see him angry, too,
   at evidences of injustice
    and mistreatment of his fellow men.
I hear him lash out
   at self-righteousness and complacency.
I watch him at last,
    when the anger is done and the sharp words said,
  stake his life on love and self-sacrifice.
I behold him die and hear him say,
    "Father, forgive them
    for they don't know what they're doing."
And, somehow, O God,
  deep inside me I know love is not weak;
   it is I who am weak.
Love is indomitable and irresistible.
Hate is weakness.
Vengeance is futile,
   and violence is self-defeating.

Help me, for it is hard
    to stand by what I do know deep inside.
It is so much easier to curse
    than to bless.
It is easier to pronounce maledictions
    than to pronounce benedictions.
It is easier to shout others down
    than to sit down with others.
It is easier to be loud
    than to listen.
O God of all people,
    who does not separate us into good and bad
        but into loving and unloving,
  I need your help lest I tear things up.
You have offered to help me, I know,
    and I hold back.
Can you push a little harder?
I want to be more loving,
    and I am afraid.

Hear my prayer.
Make my commitments to love
  more than good intentions. *Amen.*

—Kenneth G. Phifer
A Book of Uncommon Prayer

SAM'S NO-HIT, NO-RUN GAME

*B*ut I don't want to mow Mr. Mason's lawn today!" Sam argued, his blue eyes flashing.

"Sam, his mother said calmly, "you agreed to cut Mr. Mason's grass every Thursday . . . and today is Thursday."

"But Mom," he pleaded, "I gotta pitch tomorrow!"

"Yes, I know," said his mother, "but today is still Thursday."

Sam grabbed his baseball cap. He rammed it on his head so hard his curly red hair stuck out around the edges, scarecrow style. He stomped across the kitchen floor and slammed the back door.

As Sam opened Mr. Mason's gate, Augie-dog came charging across the yard like a Cincinnati Red heading for first base. With a flying leap, he landed in Sam's arms.

"You crazy little mutt," gasped Sam, protecting his right arm.

Augie-dog wiped away the last of Sam's anger with a slobbering lick across his face.

"Yuck," Sam grinned, dropping the small dog on the lawn "Come on, mutt, we've got work to do."

Pushing the mower, Sam started the endless trips around the "baseball field" sized yard. But Sam's mind was on tomorrow's game. He could see himself pawing the mound with his spiked shoes and pitching a no-hit, no-run game! And the Wildcats would be on their way to the playoffs!

Mr. Mason's call brought Sam back to reality. "Time for a break, isn't it?"

Glancing up, Sam saw Mr. Mason on the patio in his wheelchair. *I wish he was my Grandpa.* How many times had he wished that? Sam had never known either of his grandfathers, but Mr. Mason seemed like a perfect grandpa type.

Sam wiped his face on his sleeve and collapsed on the patio. "I sure could use a break."

Mr. Mason handed him a large glass of iced lemonade. Augie-dog slobbered up his cold water. Then he flopped, belly down, legs sprawled out, on the cool cement. With his head up, tongue hanging out, Augie-dog moved his alert eyes from Mr. Mason to Sam. They both laughed at his antics.

"How can you stand this mutt?" asked Sam.

"Your tough talk doesn't fool me, Sam Osborn," said Mr. Mason. "You love this little character as much as I do." He scratched Augie-dog behind the ears. "Actually, I don't know what I would do without him."

Sam's heart ached as he remembered the accident that left Mr. Mason alone and crippled. He was glad he was Mr. Mason's friend and "handyboy," and that Augie-dog was his pet.

"Well, Sam," said Mr. Mason, "I hear tomorrow's the big day. I guess a lot depends on your pitching, right?"

"Right!" replied Sam. "Reggie pitched last game and Hank has a bad elbow, so it's up to me. If we win, we'll be eligible for the playoffs!"

"Good luck," said Mr. Mason. "Why don't you finish the lawn Saturday? Got to save that arm of yours!"

"Gee thanks," cried Sam.

He gulped the remaining lemonade. He put the mower back and then zipped across the yard.

"Be sure you close the gate tight," called Mr. Mason. "Augie-dog sneaks out every chance he gets!"

On game day Sam rushed into the kitchen. He spotted his lunch and an empty glass on the table. His stomach was full of fluttering butterflies so he downed the sandwiches. He didn't bother to get any milk because he was in a hurry.

It took only a few minutes to put on his uniform. He was ready, but where was Mom?

Pausing at the full-length mirror, Sam glanced at his watch before striking a "baseball card" pose. Looking back at him was a stocky red-headed baseball star, thoughtfully holding a ball with both hands, ready to deliver an incredible pitch.

"Lookin' good," said Sam to his reflection.

He glanced at his watch again, then transformed the mirror image into a batter—feet apart, bat up and eyes focused on the incoming ball.

"Whammmn!" he exclaimed as he swung the imaginary bat.

Where's Mom?

She was his best supporter. He could always hear her voice over the crowd noises, giving him confidence and courage. Although he never said so, he needed her there, and although he would never admit it, he always glanced in her direction whenever he did anything outstanding.

He should be leaving now! The butterflies started fluttering again. *Maybe milk would help.* He headed toward the refrigerator.

"Oh, no!" cried Sam seeing the note attached to the refrigerator. It read,

> *"Sam dear, Daddy has an emergency meeting and I have to take him to the Denver airport. I won't be back until 6—Sorry I'll miss your game!—It's not too far for you to walk. Good Luck!*
> *Love You—Mom*
> *P.S. I know you'll drink your milk—so I'm putting the note here . . .*

"Oh, no!" gasped Sam. "I'll be late!"

He grabbed his spiked shoes and bounded outside.

His heart thumped hard and fast. His stomach tied into a sour knot, and he broke out in a cold sweat. *If I run real fast, I might make it.*

The sweltering sun beat down on him as he sprinted the first four blocks. "I gotta get there," he groaned. "They need me . . . I'll never make it!"

Then he remembered the shortcut. He ran across the street into the weed-filled empty lot. Something small and red caught his eye. He took a quick second look.

"Augie-dog" he gasped, recognizing the little reddish brown body covered with blood and dirt. "What happened?"

Someone left the gate open!

Augie-dog whimpered and wagged his tail feebly.

"What should I do?" Sam cried. "I can't help you . . . I'll be late . . ."

He stared at the bloody dog until hot tears blurred his focus. *Mr. Mason will find him,* he told himself. But he knew that was impossible. *But I've got to get to the game,* he thought. He turned his back on the whimpering dog and started running. Stumbling through the weeds, he remembered how much Mr. Mason loved Augie-dog. "I can't go back," he sobbed, "I just can't . . ."

At last, he could see the park, "I can still make it."

Stopping to catch his breath, the picture of Augie-dog and Mr. Mason unable to help, loomed large in his mind. "Oh, no," he cried. "What if Augie-dog dies? But I can't go back . . ." With an angry gesture, he wiped away his tears. Then he turned and rushed back to the wounded dog.

It was very late when Sam finally slipped into the Wildcats' dugout.

Reggie saw him first, "Good grief, Sam, where ya' been?" he shouted, but stopped short seeing Sam's uniform covered with dirt and blood.

The coach, hearing Sam's name, spun around with an angry look on his face. "About time you showed up."

Then he noticed Sam's uniform and said, "What happened? Were you in an accident?" he looked worried.

"Coach, something terrible happened," Sam said. "Tell you about it later. But the game, Coach? What about the game?

The dugout was unusually quiet, and Sam knew the answer.

"We lost," said the coach. "6 to 3. So, tell us about what happened to you, Sam."

Quickly Sam told them of his late start and his taking the shortcut and finding Augie-dog. As he finished he said, "So I carried Augie-dog to the vet's. Doc Vaughn said Augie-dog had been hit by a car. He had to have surgery, and Doc said he would have died if I'd gotten him there much later." Sam took a breath and continued, "I stayed until Mr. Mason came, and I knew Augie-dog would make it." With downcast eyes he added, "But, I let you guys down. It's my fault we didn't make the playoff."

A heavy silence fell over the dugout.

"Well," Coach said, "you had a tough decision to make." He picked up a towel, swung it to twist it, and said fiercely, "But if you'd done anything else, I'd have whopped you!"

For one stunned moment Sam and the team stared at the coach and then at each other. All at once the dugout exploded with laughter and rowdy roughhousing.

"Whadaya mean, it was *your* fault we lost?" shouted Reggie, "There are a few more guys on this team besides you, ya' know?"

"Yeah . . ." bellowed the Wildcats.

Relief swept over Sam. *They aren't mad at me! I did the right thing!*

"But I didn't tell you the good news," shouted Sam. "Mr. Mason was so happy that Augie-dog would be all right, he wanted to celebrate by inviting all the Wildcats to the Pizza Barn for all the pizza we can eat!"

A cheer, as loud as any victory shout, rang through the dugout. "Gee, Mr. Mason's sure a neat guy," said Hank. "Is he your grandpa or something like that?"

"Yeah," said Sam with happy grin, "something like that."

—Gerry H. Moore
Pockets

ON FRIENDSHIP

*W*hen a friendship survives many years
A lot of things go unsaid.
Like the times when I've needed so much
for someone to hear me out
and simply listen to my confusion.
And, as always, you were there—
allowing me to ramble
until the world and all its pressures
made sense.

Or the times when you came to me
to share a bit of your sorrow or joy
when for a moment you could turn to me.
How good it felt to be needed,
if only for just a while!

And if, for whatever reason,
we find we don't need each other,
I pray that we will remember
that there was a time when we did.
And a time when we might.

—David G. Broadbent
For Everything There Is a Season

Day 33

COMPASSION AND COMMITMENT

*T*o choose life is to accept the way of the cross, and sometimes it means to leave our way. I think this becomes clear in a well known text from the Gospel of Luke. It is the parable we call the "Good Samaritan." The beginning of this parable was the question addressed to Jesus, "Who is my neighbor?" The question seems good to us. It seems like the right question. And yet for Jesus it is the wrong question. "Who is my neighbor?" means this: I am in the center with *my* neighbor. "My" is first person. I am here. Please, I would like to know who *around me* is my neighbor. That was the question. "Who is my neighbor?"

You remember the parable. There were three persons: the first two were "colleagues" of mine—and then there was the third person, a Samaritan. The Samaritan leaves his way, goes to the wounded man, and the question of Jesus after was, "Which of these three men proved himself to be a neighbor to the wounded man?" It seems a little strange because spontaneously we think our neighbor is this wounded man. But the question of Jesus was, "Which of these three persons was the neighbor?" because being a neighbor is the result of our approach. Being a neighbor is a dynamic question.

One thing being a neighbor demands is that we leave our way, our present way. The neighbor is not someone whom I find in my own path but rather someone in whose path I place myself. The neighbor is not the person who is nearby. It is the distant one who is the neighbor. Or rather, the distant one will be my neighbor if I am able to approach this person, because being a neighbor is not a static question. It is the result of my action, of my commitment. We are called to be neighbors, and to be neighbors to other persons. Today I think the poor are the "distant" ones for us. They are "distant' in terms of our categories, our way of being human beings and even Christians.

We need to enter into the world of the poor. It means to leave our way today and go to the "distant one," our neighbor. And I think to try to leave our way and to make neighbors is one way to choose life. Why? Because the action of the Samaritan was to give life—in this case, health to this poor man.

As Christians we must convert the distant person into a close person through our commitment. It is a way to give life and to choose life.

—Gustavo Gutiérrez
Weavings

Excerpted from the Cole Lectures given at Vanderbilt Divinity School, January 30, 1990.

MINIATURE

*W*hat is there about making beds
that is not wasted motion?
Dust settles down
the minute I have polished.
Food prepared with such great care
is gone within an hour.

But making beds is something else,
smoothing the sheets,
fluffing the pillows,
tucking in the edges—
I am straightening the bedclothes
of a restless child,
tucking him in after prayers,
smoothing the hair from his forehead.

A woman's fingers through the years
trace images that reappear.

—Dorothy Hanson Brown
God and the Tree and Me

REMEMBER WHO YOU ARE

*W*ho Am I?
Baptism says not only that we are named and that we are royalty but also that *we are owned by God forever. . . .*

God keeps what God purchases, and on the cross an awesome price was paid.

Once God, through the church, has claimed us in baptism, God does not let us go easily. A few summers ago, a boy in our church returned home from his first year at college. He appeared at my office to tell me that I would not be seeing him at church while he was home over the summer. When I asked why, he told me, "Well, you see I have been doing a lot of thinking about religion while I was at college, and I have come to the conclusion that there is not much to this religion thing. I have found out that I don't need the church to get by," he said.

I responded by saying I found all that interesting.

"Aren't you worried? I thought you would go through the roof when I told you," he said.

I had known this boy for about five years, had baptized him a couple of years ago on profession of faith, and had watched him grow during his high school years. He came from a difficult family situation. The church had been very interested in him and had a hand in making it possible for him to go to college.

"No, I'm interested, but not overly concerned. I'll be watching to see if you can pull it off," I told him.

"What do you mean 'pull it off'? I don't understand. I'm nineteen. I can decide to do anything I want to do, can't I?"

"When I was nineteen I thought I was 'on my own,' too. I'm saying that I'm not so sure you will be able to get away with this," I said—to the increasingly confused young man.

"Why not?" he asked.

"Well, for one thing, you're baptized."

"So what does that have to do with anything?"

"Well, you try forsaking it, rejecting it, forgetting about it, and maybe you'll find out," I suggested.

"I can't figure out what being baptized has to do with me," he said.

"For one thing, there are people here who care about you. They made promises to God when you were baptized. You try not showing up around here this summer, and they will be nosing around, asking you what you are doing with your life, what kind of grades you made last semester, what you're doing with yourself. Then there's also God. No telling what God might try with you. From what I've seen of God, once he has claimed you, you don't get off the hook so easily. God is relentless in claiming what is his. And, in baptism, God says you belong to him."

The boy shook his head in wonder at this strange, unreasonable brand of ecclesiastical reasoning and more or less stumbled out the door of my study. In a week or so, he was back at his usual place on the second pew. The baptizers had done their work. God's possessiveness had remained firm. Somewhere C.S. Lewis says that he feels sorry for atheists. He feels sorry for people who try to live their lives without God, because, in Lewis's words, "God is so resourceful, so unscrupulous in keeping his own." In baptism, God tells me that he owns *me* and that he will keep me.

Remembering our baptism, we remember who we are and *whose* we are. . . .

So the church is here to remind you, to remind one another, that we have been bought with a price, that someone greater than us has named us and claimed us and

seeks us and loves us with only one good reason in mind—
so that he might love us for all eternity.

Remember *your* baptism and be thankful, for this is
who you are.

Write a prayer of thanksgiving for the person
you are, the person God has made you.

—William H. Willimon
Remember Who You Are

Week Six

✢

Times of Trial

Be gracious to me, O Lord, for I am in distress;
  my eye wastes away from grief,
  my soul and body also.

Psalm 31:9

We are afflicted in every way, but not crushed; perplexed, but not driven to despair; persecuted, but not forsaken; struck down, but not destroyed; always carrying in the body the death of Jesus, so that the life of Jesus may also be made visible in our bodies.

2 Corinthians 4:8-10

A Way to Remember

Read Colossians 3:12-17.

Whatever you do, in word or deed, do everything in the name of the Lord Jesus, giving thanks to God the Father through him.   —Colossians 3:17(RSV)

*W*e lost five of our relatives in one year to untimely deaths. I was feeling unusually depressed one morning after my husband left for work. I was gazing out the kitchen window, pondering the short lives of our loved ones. Suddenly I was aware of how fortunate I was to have this day ahead of me. I wondered what each of our loved ones would do with just one more day to live. Then I decided I would live this day doing what they would have done.

I began by baking chocolate chip cookies to welcome a new neighbor, as my mother-in-law would have done; I donated used clothing to a needy organization, as my brother would have done; I phoned a friend I had lost touch with, as my sister-in-law would have done; and I fed the birds, as my father-in-law would have done—all the while smiling as my grandchild would have.

My depression vanished, and now I live each day—with God's guidance—mindful of others who aren't here and trying to help those who are.

PRAYER: Dear Lord, please guide me in my daily work. Help me remember how fortunate I am to be alive. Amen.

THOUGHT FOR THE DAY
Live life fully.
—Nola M. Sorrells (Nebraska)
The Upper Room

Day 37

OUT OF THE DEPTHS

Psalm 130
"Out of the depths I cry to you, O Lord" (NRSV)

Introduction: This psalm is known to many by its opening words in Latin, *De profundis*—out of the depths. It is a classic penitential psalm. One can imagine the psalmist awake in the night or perhaps keeping a vigil in the Temple, waiting for the Lord's help, more eagerly than watchmen wait for the dawn. It is both a powerful statement of the human condition and a joyful acknowledgment of God's love, which is stronger than death. It is one of the most magnificent statements of faith in the Psalter, declaring profound hope, even in the midst of profound despair.

Preparation: As we prepare for prayer, it is not necessary to ask for God to be present to us. It is only necessary to put aside our distractions so that *we can be present to God* who is already as close as our breath.

Read Psalm 130: This is a psalm worth reading again and again, perhaps in different translations. Read it and pray it, until finally, the psalm prays itself.

Reflection: "From the depths of my despair" (TEV). Rare is the person who has not been there. Recall a time of your own despair. What feelings did you have about God as you struggled through it? Anger? Abandonment? Apathy?

Prayer: Pray for the gift of being open to God's
presence in your life, even when you cry
"out of the depths."

—Donald E. Collins
Like Trees That Grow Beside a Stream

Day 38

OF SEEDS AND SUFFERING

*F*eelings of failure, shame, guilt, and worthlessness tangled together. I felt abandoned and unwanted. I felt pain as I had never felt before and, at the same time, I felt nothing.

I wrestled with the meaning of reconciliation. If I were truly a person of faith, shouldn't I be reconciled with my husband? Wouldn't that mean returning to the marriage? If I had faith, wouldn't "all things" be "possible" —even to the healing of gaping wounds and deep differences? Wouldn't faith make it possible to forgive and love again? I had once committed myself to working on the relationship, to saving the marriage. Why was I now feeling it was better that it end? Why, on that day I finally slipped my wedding band from my finger, did I feel such relief, such lifting of burden?

Our marriage had withered and died. My life faded like an aging flower, dropping petal by petal to the earth. The challenge of that death was embracing my brokenness as an invitation to wholeness, not defeat. Something deep inside subtly pushed me to seek new life. A slender thread of hope remained. In the turmoil, my faith was stripped of platitudes, easy answers, simplicities. I grappled with the rawness of life. If my faith didn't count here, it wouldn't count anywhere. But I still felt defeated and wearily battled despair. I was challenged to be when I felt there was no reason to be, when I felt I was nothing. And I was challenged to pray when I felt I could not pray. Gone was my ability to gather my prayers into a coherent whole. Gone was my ability to think, to center. I cried from the depths of my aching heart. The Spirit groaned with me. Over and over I cried, "Help me, hear me, hold me, heal me." At times God's presence was palpable, but more often I felt utterly alone. Yet it was when I felt most powerless and most alone that prayer became deeper than words, deeper than understanding. Words cannot express the silent embrace of God. I lost control of my life; I was deeply vulnerable (from Latin *vulnus,* wound), woundable. Ironically, I was also healable. With my defenses gone, God could, perhaps for the first time ever, come fully into my life.

"Tears are a sign of the presence of God," an early Christian writer asserted. Tears I knew well. And in my tears, I came to know the compassionate God. As a child in Sunday school, I had heard stories of a loving God. Yet my experiences of God, interpreted by an authoritarian father, were of judgment and vengeance. Now in my pain, that God of love was touching me and melting away old images from my heart. I did not quite trust it at first: How could God love me so much to have such compassion? And yet, if God was compassionate, why was I suffering?

In my barrenness, the richness of ritual reassured and sustained me. I hungered for the sacrament of life. Each Eucharist became a plea for healing, a cry for life. My ability to control and shape my life was gone. Ritual, empowered by the Spirit, provided a form to express the formless void I felt within. I could not create new prayers. Singing the psalms and litanies that the faithful had sung for ages gave voice as well as context to my pain. Endless numbers of people had cried out to God in ritual and symbol; now I joined them. Empowered and empowering, ritual and symbol became shorthand script for the steadfast presence of God. During my trauma, tradition and ritual became tap roots that helped sustain life.

—Jean M. Blomquist
Weavings

RABBITS IN WINTER

*Y*ou probably don't know my rabbits.
They moved here from Vermont in a box last July. Some boy was handing them out on the street and all three of my children sat down in front of the box as we walked by. The sign said free rabbits. The kids said sit-down strike.

I thought it was fine to have rabbits outdoors in the summer, but I was scared about the winter. I didn't want them in the house. Then somebody told me about the way rabbits grow fur. They grow it as the temperature demands. This no doubt is yet another piece of the majesty of God, putting fasteners on the seas, morning lights in the sky, fur on the rabbits.

Take a family that gets into crisis: a child that fails to thrive or goes on drugs. The day the tragedy announces itself the family does not have what they need to cope. When they tell you they don't know how they are going to cope, you have to agree. They don't know. Yet, their fur hasn't grown. But what we see—in the parents' support groups of a thousand hospitals—is fur growing, capacity increasing. Our strength is made manifest in struggle. Our growth occurs because of the struggle. The fur grows in response to winter slowly and surely. The bread comes to us day by day.

I see this in my personal life all the time. I'll say enough. I'll shout too much. God won't say much back. And then I'll find a new opening at the bottom of my well. A new capacity to take risks. A renewed capacity to love and forgive. A crevice when I thought there were no more places to go to feed on the tree.

I have often heard it said: "First you jump. Then you get your wings." In the deep of winter our fur grows. Our capacity to handle trouble grows with the trouble.

—Donna Schaper
alive now!

Day 40
(Palm Sunday)

WHEN LONELINESS DOES NOT GO AWAY

*R*ead: Luke 19:28-41.
It is what one writer described as "feeling like a cuckoo in a nest of swallows."

A young professional man put it this way: "You want to put your head on someone's lap and feel a closeness that is not physical or mental but spiritual."

A woman in her middle years confessed: "There have been many times when I felt it so desperately that I have gone to the greeting card rack and bought for myself the card I wished someone had sent me."

One man yearns so much to have someone speak to him that he dials his telephone to hear a recorded voice say, "The time is. . . . "

We live in an age of alienation and loneliness. Some suggest it is a loneliness of soul such as never existed before. It affects young and old, rich and poor, strong and weak. Those who live alone experience it and so do those who are surrounded by family and friends. A recent study indicated that the loneliest of persons can be married couples—people with nice homes, good jobs, money, family activities, and all the rest, but who are out of touch with each other, who have no intimacy or mutual understanding. None of us is entirely free of loneliness, and many are desperately lonely.

There is a loneliness about that first Palm Sunday. You sense and feel it in Jesus as the donkey on which he is riding clops along the sunbaked, dusty road. Amidst the shouting and singing of the crowd, the dancing, the children running and waving palm branches, and the people craning their necks to get a better look, he rides. He rides in loneliness, because he knows most of the people have no idea what is actually going on and care less. He knows that they do not know or understand. His knowing is the pain of loneliness. At the descent of the Mount of Olives, he stops, looks across the Kidron Valley at Jerusalem, now visible in panoramic view. He weeps!

There is loneliness in the crowd, too. That is why they have come to what they think is a parade, hoping something might happen to interrupt their aimlessness, hoping the entertainment will fill their inner emptiness. They have come looking for more than crowd excitement, although they may not be aware of it. They have come because they yearn for community and connection. This Jesus of Nazareth may finally be the Messiah who will improve their lot in life and give them a sense of belonging.

Two thousand years later, we still search for community and crave a sense of belonging. We want relationships that confer meaning and give purpose to life. Our loneliness is the desire to be home, to have a place, to be with persons who care and are willing to come close. Without such relationships, we live in half-worlds.

Love is constancy—the constancy we see in Jesus, who, "having loved his own who were in the world, he loved them to the end" (John 13:1), even when they misunderstood him, tried to dissuade him, denied him, and forsook him. Jesus never yielded or compromised the responsibilities of love. Although it meant being treated as a stranger of no address, he stayed open to God's revelation dwelling in him. He drew persons near with reverence and care, and with concern and trust he held before them a vision, waking them to God's claim. He walked with persons and by his presence encouraged them to risk greatness and forsake littleness. "You are of great worth" (Matt. 10:31, my paraphrase); "You are the light of the world" (Matt. 5:14); "As I have loved you, . . . you also love one another" (John 13:34).

There is a risk of loneliness for us when we believe in and care about persons, when we keep on believing in and caring for them. They may reject us, impugn the very love we give to them, make inordinate demands upon us, and even violate our trust. That has been, however, is now, and always will be the cost of discipleship. . . .

He who knew loneliness comes to us in ours. He who was forsaken does not forsake us. He is still on the premises with love.

—Donald J. Shelby
Meeting the Messiah

MIDNIGHT INVOCATION

Only the darkness is whole. All else seems
chipped, hollow, tarnished, ragged, spilled, or
teetering on the brink. Even the silver mirror of
sleep lies shattered.
But you, Lord, having knelt in dark,
sharp-edged places, *you know.* So I've gathered them
up, Lord, these fragments of words, tears, love,
need, pain—more than twelve baskets full. You take
them. Once again, reach your hand into humanity
and bless the broken.

—Barbara Seaman
alive now!

JESUS STRUGGLES WITH US

As you read through the Passion narratives, you
will find that these events are loaded with very
real, very normal, very predictable human
emotions. This is the stuff of your life and mine.
Jesus says to the disciples, "My heart is so weighted down
with grief and sorrow that it almost crushes me." We
understand this. All of us face those moments of grief and
disappointment which weigh heavily upon us and almost
crush the life out of us.

We can hear Jesus struggle in prayer with God,
searching for some other way through: "Father, if there is
any way possible to get me out of this mess, get me out of

it!" There are times in all our lives when, confronted by the circumstances and realities around us, we cry out, "God, give me an escape hatch! Get me out of this!" Jesus experiences this with us.

—James A. Harnish
What Will You Do with King Jesus?

Un Sacrificio de Amor

Léase Juan 19:17-30.

Porque de tal manera amó Dios al mundo, que ha
dado a su Hijo unigénito, para que todo aquel que
en Él cree, no se pierda, más tenga vida eterna.
—Juan 3:16 (VRV)

C uando Jesús abrió mis ojos y mi entendimiento y
pude comprender el precioso sacrificio que Él
hizo en la cruz al dar Su vida por mí, empecé a
llorar.

Y mientras más pensaba en ese sufrimiento suyo—
en Su agonía—más lloraba.

Me preguntaba una y otra vez, quién era yo para
que un ser inocente como Él muriera por mí.

En los días subsiquientes vertí muchas lágrimas.

Pero después experimenté una sensación que antes
no había sentido. Sentí una seguridad completa y un gozo
inmenso por ese amore tan grande que Jesús había
demostrado por mí al morir en las cruz.

Desde ese momento tuve la certeza de que Jesús
estaba conmigo dirigiendo mi vida; dispuesto a continuar
bregando conmigo.

Cristo Jesús nos revela que Él verdaderamente nos
ama y continuamente está velando por nosotros, siempre
dispuesto a perdonarnos y ayudarnos.

Extiéndele tú tu mano a Él, pídele conocerlo, y Él te
responderá.

ORACIÓN: Señor Jesús, gracias por ese sacrificio Tuyo por cada uno de nosotros. Ayúdanos a entender cuál es Tu voluntad para nuestra vida. Amén.

PENSAMIENTO PARA EL DÍA
Dios nos revela Su amor inefable cada día.

Sra. Palmira S. Oliveras (San Germán, Puerto Rico)
El Aposento Alto

A SACRIFICE OF LOVE

Read John 19: 17-30.

For God so loved the world that he gave his only Son, that whoever believes in him should not perish but have eternal life.   —John 3:16

*I*t was the moment when Christ opened my eyes and my understanding that I was able to fathom the incredible sacrifice He made on the cross for me, and I began to cry.

The more I thought of that personal sacrifice for me and the anguish of His death, I wept even more. I could not stop questioning whether I was worth the price of an innocent person's death.

In the days following this experience, I continued to cry as I thought of this. But then came a time when I felt completely certain of the love Jesus had shown for me on the cross, and I was swept by an incredible joy.

I was filled with the certainty that Jesus was in me, leading my life and willing to continue to be with me in my struggles.

PRAYER: Lord Jesus, thank you for sacrificing your life for each of us. Help us to discern what is your will for our lives. Amen.

THOUGHT FOR THE DAY
Every day, Jesus reveals His love for us.

Mrs. Palmira S. Oliveras (San Germán, Puerto Rico)
El Aposento Alto
Translated by Horacio M. Ríos

Week Seven

Through the Darkness
Into the Light

So they took Jesus; and carrying the cross by himself, he went out to what is called The Place of the Skull, which in Hebrew is called Golgotha. There they crucified him.

John 19:16-18

The angel said to the women, "Do not be afraid; I know that you are looking for Jesus who was crucified. He is not here; for he has been raised, as he said."

Matthew 28:5-6

For once you were in darkness, but now in the Lord you are light. Live as children of light.

Ephesians 5:8

JUDAS ISCARIOT

*R*ead John 13:18-30.
I am Judas bar Simon. I'm from the town Kerioth, in Galilee. One of Jesus' brothers is called Judas, too, so some call me Judas Iscariot. Judas is a common name.

I have been traveling with Jesus for over two years, and I really thought he was the one. Many of us did, and I thought we were going to succeed. A few days ago the people were ready to make him king—but he wouldn't let them. He is throwing over our cause, and we are all going to look like fools.

I don't think he understands. He's an idealist, a dreamer. He believes absolutely in what he's doing. The healings and the teaching are fine as far as they go, but that's the place to begin, not the place to stop. I've tried to tell him you can't change the world just one person at a time. You have to deal with the bigger issues. I really thought God was going to use him to restore the kingdom to Israel. But if he won't take the reins politically, he can't change the system. The time is right for us to act now, but he stands in the way of building any other widespread alliance. As wonderful as he is, he has become a liability, too.

The authorities would like to see Jesus out of the picture, and I think I've figured out a way to use that: I am going to turn Jesus over to them. They're stupid. They don't realize what making him a martyr will do for us. It's a desperate move, but this is a time for desperate measures.

Sometimes there are things that are bigger than one person. I really believe Jesus loves his ideals enough to die for them. Maybe the time has come for that. Maybe.

Suggestion for meditation: *At what places in your life is Jesus not what you want? How do you deal with that?*

—Mary Lou Redding
The Upper Room Disciplines 1992

NOT SERVANTS BUT FRIENDS

No longer do I call you servants, for the servant does not know what his master is doing; but I have called you friends, for all that I have heard from my father I have made known to you.
—John 15:15 (RSV)

*J*esus speaks these words to his disciples on his way out of the world. Anticipating his death, he gathers them together for one last supper and tries to tell them everything they will need to know: about the world, about themselves, about himself and God. According to John, it takes him four whole chapters to say good-bye—four chapters full of instructions, laments, warnings, and assurances. Like a parent leaving town, he is brimming with love and anxiety for those he leaves behind: be careful, look after each other, remember your chores, and don't worry about me; everything will be all right, you'll see.

Part of what his disciples need to know, apparently, is who they are. In the past they have been his recruits, looking to him for direction and following his lead. They have accompanied him from town to town and supported his ministry; they have hung on his words and been sustained by his vision, but always they have drawn a clear line between who they are and who he is. However much they have grown in his company, they are his followers and he is their leader; they are his students and he is their teacher.

He is the one with direct access to God, the one with the divine plan and the know-how to make it happen.

He is the one in charge, the one to whom they report and from whom they get their orders. He is the Lord; they are servants of the Lord—at least until it comes time for him to say good-bye. That is when Jesus, in his thoroughly startling way, announces to his disciples that their apprenticeship is over. They know everything he knows; he has nothing more to teach them. They are no longer his servants but his friends.

On his way out of the world, what he needs are companions willing to pick up where he leaves off, partners able to adopt his ministry as their own. On the road toward his own passion, what he needs is their compassion—their willingness to suffer with him, to bear part of his burden, to share his hopes and fears. What he needs are not servants but friends.

It should have been good news, as it should be good news to every one of us that we are baptized into God's household not as slaves, but as heirs, heirs of God and fellow heirs with Christ. It should be good news that we are received into God's service as friends, to carry on Christ's work of reconciliation in the world. It should be good news that we are called into compassion with him to minister in his name—each according to the gifts given us— but I wonder. I wonder if some of us would not really rather decline the honor and stay put in the servants' quarters.

There is a lot to be said for being a servant, after all. Someone else makes the decisions and carries the responsibility. Someone else runs the show. All I have to do is follow orders. I can be loyal and reliable and polish the silver better than anyone else; I can do more than I am asked and never complain, but when push comes to shove I can hang up my apron and go home. Being a servant means doing a job for someone else; it means taking a subordinate role. So let someone else save the world; I just work here. . . .

But being a friend is much harder than being a servant. You are self-employed, for one thing; there is no one to tell you what to do or how to do it. You are left to your own devices, and there is no pay for overtime—which is just as well, since the hours are highly irregular. Being a friend means taking time out on the busiest day of your life to hold someone's hand while he waits in the doctor's office and talking to him on the telephone in the middle of the night when he wakes up afraid. It means agonizing with someone over her decision to leave her job and celebrating with her when she finds a new one. Being a friend means saying, "I will go with you" over and over again, whether you feel like it or not. It means caring about people so much that you get your hopes and fears all mixed up with their own, and that you want the best for them as much as you want it for yourself.

At his last supper, that is who Jesus wants around him, and who he wants to carry on in his name—not slaves, who follow his orders without a clue as to what he means; nor servants, who do their jobs and go home; but compassionate friends, who accept his ministry as their own and take responsibility for it, risks and all.

It is not something we are ever ready to do. Jesus can prepare us for four full chapters—sharing his dreams with us, confiding his purposes, telling us everything he knows—and still we are likely to play ignorant at the end, partly because we are afraid we will fail at our task and partly because we are afraid we will succeed. Everything we know about friendship with God prepares us for the worst: will we be stuffed down a cistern like Jeremiah or burned at the stake like Joan? Beaten to death in prison like Stephen Biko or gunned down at the altar like Archbishop Romero?

"No wonder you have so few friends if this is how you treat them," Teresa of Avila scolded her Lord in the sixteenth century, and it is no different today. The exercise of compassion is strenuous enough with our earthbound friends, but to be God's friend is to enter into relationship with the creator of heaven and earth, a relationship in which there is no room for calculated risks or guarantees of safety. To be God's friend is to plunge right into the darkest mysteries of the universe and to swim toward the light, taking as much of the world to the surface with you as you can.

To be Christ's friend is to sit with him on the last day of his life—or on any day of your own—and to listen to him, sharing his hopes and fears, claiming his vision as your own and accepting his invitation of friendship, knowing full well where he is headed and saying, as all good friends do, "I will go with you."

It is not something we are ever ready to do, which is why Jesus reminds us that we did not choose him. "I chose you," he says, "and appointed you that you should go and bear fruit and that your fruit should abide . . ." (John 15:16, RSV). If we show compassion, it is because we have been shown compassion. If we are related to him at all, it is not because we have chosen him but because he has chosen us—not for our brains, not for our beauty, and certainly not for our faithfulness—but simply because he has chosen us: not to be his servants but to be his friends.

—Barbara Brown Taylor
Weavings

40 Days

The journey
From a listless Lent
Towards an exhilarating Easter
Requires this length of time
To discover again
That amazing Love
Makes
Friday "Good."

—Ken Fansler
alive now!

Good Friday

*J*esus is on the cross. Our rebellion, our self-enthronement, our desire to be God put him there. And each time we give in to self-will, to self-centered ways of living, we drive the nails deeper; we "crucify" the Son of God afresh and "put him to an open shame" (Heb. 6:6, KJV). In your mind, place yourself in the crowd around the cross of Jesus. Let the reality of the consequences of human sin—your sin—be driven home to you. What are the sins in your life which form the thorns in his crown or the nails in his hands?

You may find it deeply meaningful to spend the hours between noon and 3:00 P.M. in silence and in meditation if circumstances permit. Or, perhaps you will be able to attend a three-hour Good Friday service. By giving this extended time to meditate on the meaning of Jesus' death for us, you will greatly enrich your observance. You might find it helpful to structure your three-hour time of meditation around the words of Jesus on the cross. You would need to look at the crucifixion story in all the Gospels to include all seven "words."

The cross is not only the symbol of death but also the symbol of life, for on it Jesus bore the destruction that our sins and our self-centered lives should have brought upon us. So as you wait at the cross today, mourn the sins that put him there but also "feel his blood applied," as Charles Wesley so aptly put it. Let today truly become *Good* Friday for you.

—Larry R. Kalajainen
A Lenten Journey

THE HEART OF CHRISTIAN PARADOX

*R*ead Matthew 28:1-10.
Among the significant variations in the Gospel accounts of the Resurrection, Matthew alone offers dramatic details of an earthquake and guards struck dumb by the lightening-faced glory of an angel. It is the evangelist's way of expressing the most incomprehensible, shattering event ever recorded.

The confusion, fear, joy, and disbelief revealed in the responses of the women and later the disciples are natural human reactions to a reality which feels impossible. In the same way that we become numbed by sudden tragedy, we can be numbed into disbelief by events that seem too good to be true. The living Jesus standing before his followers must have seemed a precious and fragile dream, a gift which could vanish in a moment's waking.

The brutal realities of crucifixion can feel much more real to us than the realities of resurrection. The politics of Jewish leaders with Pilate, bribing witnesses to conceal the truth (vv. 11-15)—these are believable enough. But life recreated out of pure agony? Warmth and light from the stone-cold tomb? To accept the Resurrection is to awaken into God's kingdom—a realm where, contrary to our experience, life is not defeated by death. To recognize the Resurrection is to awake in a new kind of morning, one in which the bleak human landscape of sin seems more the fading dream than encompassing reality. In its eternal light a whole new order of life is born.

Suggestion for prayer: *Imagine yourself one of the women or disciples being greeted by the risen Lord. What are your feelings?*

What would it mean to accept the reality of resurrection in your life right now?

—Marjorie J. Thompson
The Upper Room Disciplines 1990

EASTER MORNING

*D*espite the growing shadow of Idi Amin, Easter morning, 1973, began as a most joyous occasion for the Redeemed Church. The sun had just risen and the sky was empty of clouds when the first people began arriving at the compound where we worshiped. They came from almost every tribe, from the Baganda, the Basoga, the Banyankole, the Acholi and the Langi, the Bagweri and the Bagisu. They came from as far away as Masaka, a town eighty miles southwest of Kampala. There were old men with walking sticks and young women with babies on their backs. There were small children with flowers in their arms. There were doctors and lawyers, businessmen and farmers, cotton growers and government workers. Only a few had traveled by private car or taxi. Most came on foot or rode bicycles. Others crowded into lorries so lopsided they seemed ready to collapse at any moment. But however the people traveled, they arrived with the same joyful greeting "Aleluya, Azukide! Hallelujah, He is risen!"

By 9:00 over 7,000 people were gathered. It was the largest crowd ever to attend Sunday service at the Redeemed Church. When there were no more places in the compound, people climbed trees or sat on the roofs of parked lorries. A few large groups set up in nearby yards with their own amplifying systems. Hundreds of others stood in the street.

Before the service, the elders and I met in the "vestry," an empty house by the compound to pray. We felt deeply the hunger in the hearts of the people who had gathered for worship. We knew their desire to hear the

Word of God and we prayed that their lives would be transformed by its power. As we poured our hearts out to the Father in agonizing intercession, desperate scenes from the previous weeks flashed again in my mind. I saw a face burned beyond recognition, and a woman huddled in a corner weeping. I saw a crowd of soldiers standing in the park cheering, and heard the sound of boot crunching against bone. I remembered the arrogance of the mercenaries, and the dreamlike deadness of my heart. Once again the triumph of evil overwhelmed me. I felt a deep fear. I myself had fallen, how could I hope to strengthen others? Who was I to feed God's children in this most desperate hour? What words could I speak? My brothers and sisters needed courage to stand firm in the growing terror. They needed strength to sustain them in suffering. They did not need my sermon. They did not need my thoughts on the Resurrection. My father had been right. "In such times men do not need words, " he had said. "They need power."

As I prayed for strength and wisdom, the words of Matthew 14:19 came to my mind. It was the same text that a brother from the Revival Fellowship had read to me many years before.

And taking the five loaves and the two fish he looked up to heaven, and blessed, and broke and gave the loaves to the disciples, and the disciples gave them to the crowds.

With this verse, I heard the convicting voice of the Holy Spirit. It was Jesus who provided bread for the crowds. The disciples' task was only to distribute what their Master had already given them. It was God who sustained His people. He was not asking me to feed His children from the words of my own heart. He was only asking me to distribute the living bread He had put into my hand.

I closed the service with the benediction. In the uncertainty of our lives and with the nearness of death, the words of Simeon held deep meaning:

Lord, now lettest thou thy servant depart in peace, according to thy word; for mine eyes have seen thy salvation, which thou hast prepared before the face of all people.

We did not know when we would see each other again or when God might call us home. But we went out in peace because we had seen with our eyes the salvation of the Lord. With a loud amen from the people and a final chorus from the choir the Easter service ended. I turned to the elders and we embraced, praising God. It seemed as if days instead of hours had passed since we had met for prayer. I was exhausted, but there was joy in my heart. God had answered our prayers: He had broken bread and fed His people.

I greeted several more friends and then left for the vestry to change my clothes, hoping to have a few minutes alone in prayer. I had to push my way through the crowd and when I finally arrived at the house I was exhausted. I was too tired to notice the men behind me until they had closed the door.

There were five of them. They stood between me and the door, pointing their rifles at my face. Their own faces were scarred with the distinctive tribal cuttings of the Kahwa tribe. They were dressed casually in flowered shirts and bell-bottom pants, and wore sunglasses. Although I had never seen any of them before, I recognized them immediately. They were the secret police of the State Research Bureau—Amin's Nubian assassins.

For a long moment no one said anything. Then the tallest man, obviously the leader, spoke. "We are going to kill you," he said. "If you have something to say, say it before you die." He spoke quietly but his face was twisted with hatred.

I could only stare at him. For a sickening moment I felt the full weight of his rage. We had never met before but his deepest desire was to tear me to pieces. My mouth felt heavy and my limbs began to shake. Everything left my control. "They will not need to kill me," I thought to myself. "I am just going to fall over. I am going to fall over dead and I will never see my family again." I thought of Penina home alone with Damali. What would happen to them when I was gone?

From far away I heard a voice, and I was astonished to realize that it was my own. "I do not need to plead my own cause," I heard myself saying. "I am a dead man already. My life is dead and hidden in Christ. It is your lives that are in danger, you are dead in your sins. I will pray to God that after you have killed me, He will spare you from eternal destruction."

The tallest one took a step towards me and then stopped. In an instant, his face was changed. His hatred had turned to curiosity. He lowered his gun and motioned to the others to do the same. They stared at him in amazement but they took their guns from my face.

Then the tall one spoke again. "Will you pray for us now?" he asked.

"Yes, I will pray for you," I answered. My voice sounded bolder even to myself. "I will pray to the Father in heaven. Please bow your heads and close your eyes."

The tall one motioned to the others again, and together the five of them lowered their heads. I bowed my own head, but I kept my eyes open. The Nubian's request seemed to me a strange trick. Any minute, I thought to myself, my life will end. I did not want to die with my eyes closed.

"Father in heaven," I prayed, "you who have forgiven men in the past, forgive these men also. Do not let them perish in their sins but bring them into yourself."

It was a simple prayer, prayed in deep fear. But God looked beyond my fears and when I lifted my head, the men standing in front of me were not the same men who had followed me into the vestry. Something had changed in their faces.

It was the tall one who spoke first. His voice was bold but there we no contempt in his words. "You have helped us," he said, "and we will help you. We will speak to the rest of our company and they will leave you alone. Do not fear for your life. It is in our hands and you will be protected."

I drove home that Easter evening deeply puzzled but with joy in my heart. I felt that I had passed from death to life, and that I could now speak in one mind with Paul:

I have been crucified with Christ and I no longer live, but Christ lives in me. The life I live in the body, I live by faith in the Son of God, who loved me and gave himself for me.

Later the assassins began attending Sempangi's church and claimed a new commitment to Jesus Christ. They used their positions to help church members whose lives were in danger, and even helped several families escape from Uganda.

—Kefa Sempangi
Weavings

Reprinted as in *Weavings* from *A Distant Grief* by Kefa Sempangi © 1979. Regal Books, Ventura, CA 93003. Used by permission.

AN EASTER LITANY

The women came running to tell us.
>**Christ is risen**
>**Christ is risen, indeed.**

Out of darkness, light has come.
>**Christ is risen**
>**Christ is risen, indeed.**

The tomb is empty, our hearts are full.
>**Christ is risen**
>**Christ is risen, indeed**

Our mourning has been turned to dancing.
>**Christ is risen**
>**Christ is risen, indeed.**

Our tears have been turned to laughter.
>**Christ is risen**
>**Christ is risen, indeed.**

The stone moved away from the door of the tomb.
>**Christ is risen**
>**Christ is risen, indeed.**

Captives at liberty, prisoners set free.
>**Christ is risen**
>**Christ is risen, indeed.**

Death clothes cast aside to bind up broken hearts.
>**Christ is risen**
>**Christ is risen, indeed.**

The lowly are lifted, the mighty brought down.
>**Christ is risen**
>**Christ is risen, indeed.**

Today the promise of God is fulfilled in our hearing.
>**Christ is risen**
>**Christ is risen, indeed.**
>**Alleluia! Alleluia!**

—Michael E. Williams
alive now!

THE WOMEN

*A*s I was reflecting on the events of the first Easter, my ten-year-old daughter, Katie, came into the room and began bugging me, as she sometimes likes to do when she knows I'm trying to concentrate.

We got to chatting about what I was working on, and just for fun, I asked, "Who were the ones who first knew Jesus had been raised from the dead?"

Somewhat to my surprise she said, "The women."

So I asked a follow-up question, "Why the women?"

And Katie said, "Because women take care of things."

—Kenneth L. Gibble
alive now!

After Easter

OUR OWN GALILEE

Read Matthew 28:1-10.

Jesus said to them, "Do not be afraid; go and tell my brethren to go to Galilee, and there they will see me."
—Matthew 28:10 (RSV)

*A*t the empty tomb the risen Lord urged the two Marys not to be afraid and to tell the disciples where to go to see him. For many of Jesus' closest followers, the reality and power of His resurrection took form on a mountain in Galilee rather than at the garden tomb.

It is comforting to know that Easter can also become real to us in other places. Sometimes I need to hear those words of Jesus to the two women. I need Jesus to calm my fears and tell me where to boldly go to experience the new life of the resurrection. That place may be a broken relationship or a frightening situation, a moral decision or a private battle with boredom or depression. We each have our own "Galilee" where the risen Christ awaits us.

No matter where our individual Galilees are, Christ has gone before us and urges us to be unafraid. We are to go to the broken places in our lives, trusting that Christ will be there to meet us.

PRAYER: O Lord, help me to find the power of the Resurrection in the uncertain and painful corners of my life. I pray trusting in Christ who calls me. Amen.

THOUGHT FOR THE DAY
Wherever I am today, I have access to the power of Christ.
—Dan Moore (New York)
The Upper Room

136 ❖ *After Easter*

PUTTING ON CHRIST

For almost six years Dale came to see me once a month for spiritual direction. During that time, he moved through exciting adventures with God that influenced every aspect of his life. One fall he was diagnosed with cancer.

As the disease progressed, Dale and I talked about the issues one faces when death is imminent: finances, funeral arrangements, leave-taking. One of our visits during his final weeks took place at his home. He was still working as an ophthalmologist for a while in the morning, coming home to rest and then going back to the office in the afternoon. On this particular day, he was lying on his bed resting and we were talking about what the next life would be like. He spoke of his grief at leaving his wife, children, and friends, yet he looked forward to being reunited with young Dale, his son who had died some years before. Then getting off the bed, he eased into a chair and we sat face-to-face. From out of nowhere, Dale asked, "What size suit do you wear, Ron?"

"Forty regular."

"Would you mind wearing someone else's clothes?"

"No. Why?"

"Because after I'm dead, you're going to have some nice clothes." With great effort, Dale got up and walked over to his closet. Pulling out sleeves of his suits and jackets, he reminded me of a salesperson as he said, "You'll look good in this . . . this is a good color . . . this is a wonderful fabric." Then he pulled out a gray herringbone sportcoat. "When you wear this, I want you to remember that it was my favorite."

Dale had always stood out as being especially well dressed and now *he was leaving his clothes to me!* I stood there stunned and groped for words to express my feelings. Already grieving the loss of this good and kind friend, all I could manage to say was, "Thank you so much, Dale. I'm touched and honored."

Dale dismissed my gratitude with a wave of his hand. "What size shoe do you wear?"

"Nine and a half . . . or ten."

"Can't help you there. I'm an eight and a half."

"Tell you what," I said, "you provide the suits and I'll provide the shoes." We laughed together for what turned out to be the last time.

The following week was Holy Week. Saddened as I was at the prospect of losing a friend, Dale's gift helped me find new meaning in the death and resurrection of Jesus.

One problem I've always had with the death of Jesus—and I suspect this is true for a lot of Christians—is that it doesn't seem real. When I was in Nicaragua and listened to some of the mothers who had seen their sons and daughters killed, I got physically ill just hearing about the barbarity. Yet I can conduct a Holy Week service in which the passion of our Lord Jesus Christ is read and I am not deeply affected. Perhaps this is because the crucifixion happened some 2,000 years ago and time has distanced us from it emotionally. After my experience in Nicaragua, I decided that each Holy Week I was going to look for a symbol or image that spoke to me in a personal way about Jesus' death and resurrection. This year Dale's gift provided me with what I was looking for.

Five days after my last visit with Dale, I preached at a small celebration of the Eucharist during Holy Week. After telling about my friendship with Dale and the gift of his clothes, I said, "When I put on one of Dale's jackets or a pair of his slacks, I'm going to remember that he was a gracious, gentle man who loved his family and was loyal to his friends. I'm going to recall that he was honorable in all his dealings and dedicated himself to working for social justice. I'll also remember that he suffered a painful death and now lives a new, risen life. What is true of Dale is also true of Jesus. I believe that Dale's life serves as a example of what it means to put on the mind of Christ. "I concluded by saying, "Each time I put on Dale's clothing, I will remind myself to also put on Christ—to live as he did and to do as he did. Dale's life, death, and passage to risen life will be a symbol for me of the death and resurrection of Jesus."

Dale died shortly after Easter, and I later received his clothing. Since then I've worn something of his nearly every day. And when I do, I remember.

—Ron DelBene
From the Heart

COME

*J*esus,
Who wakened
On that Easter morning,
Come, waken me
Come, waken me.

—Thomas John Carlisle
alive now!

Appendix

QUESTIONS FOR DISCUSSION

ABOUT THE AUTHORS

QUESTIONS FOR DISCUSSION

Week One: A Time of Preparation
Day 1: Phyllis Tickle speaks of Lent as a time of inactivity that precedes the excess and wastefulness of spring. Do you think of Lent as a time of dullness, of inactivity? If not, how would you characterize this season? If Lent is a time of inactivity, how does this season help prepare us for the Resurrection and the "absurd wastefulness of spring"?

Day 2: To be "refurbished within" is a request we might make especially during the Lenten season. Kenneth Phifer speaks of this kind of transformation as something that can affect both the mind and the heart. What are the areas in your life that need to be refurbished and redecorated?

Day 3: Lent is a time when we think naturally of the wilderness, for wilderness is often associated with a time of testing. What wilderness experiences have you known in your life? How have these been places for renewal as well as places of testing?

Day 4: By his example, Brother Lawrence, the "kitchen saint," taught us to recognize the presence of God in the everyday. When during this past week were you especially aware of God's presence? Practice seeing God in the everyday this coming week.

Day 5: Jesus' statement about loving our life and losing it, and hating our life and keeping it for eternal life is confusing and perhaps unsettling. The author explains that it is only when we are willing to die to ourselves that we will be able to see Jesus. What does it mean to you to "die to yourself"? How can that be a positive idea and not a self-denigrating one?

Day 6: Rueben Job talks about something we all do from time to time—we push away from the embrace of God. But just as a newborn infant needs the embrace of its loving parent, we need the embrace of God. How have you felt God's embrace this week? When were times you pushed away from that embrace? Why did you push away? Try to pay attention to God's embrace during the week to come.

Day 7: Try the journaling exercise in Day 7. Choose another scripture passage if you want to. Let those who want to, read aloud what they have written.

Week Two: To Forgive and Be Forgiven
Day 8: In the story about the man who had contracted a rare form of cancer, the author says that many of us look for cause-and-effect relationships to explain why bad things happen to people. Why do we have this tendency? What is a better way to respond to such tragedies?

Day 9: Kenneth Phifer expresses the desire that he would be able to come to God, not only with his "morning face and eager heart," but with his "tears and aches." Are you more reluctant to talk to God when you're not feeling "up"? Why?

Day 10: The author of "Redemption" says that "sorrow carved into my heart a large capacity for joy and peace which walk hand in hand with redemptive love." She was able to see God's grace at work even through a wounded childhood. Are there areas of your life where God has worked for good in your life in the midst of wounding circumstances?

Day 11: The authors compare the experiences of Judas and Peter: Judas sinned, repented, and yet was unable to believe that God still loved him. Peter sinned, repented, and accepted God's love and forgiveness. Do you ever close God's love and forgiveness out and seek to punish yourself? How does God seek you out during those times?

Day 12: Let someone in the group read aloud this meditation from Flora Slosson Wuellner, while the other members of the group close their eyes and participate. Make sure every person knows that he or she does not have to participate if the meditation becomes too painful or threatening.

Day 13: Scott found it very difficult to make the first move toward reconciliation with his friend Jeff, especially since he saw Jeff as being the one who offended him. Do you have a relationship that needs reconciliation? How can you make the first move?

Day 14: The author makes the statement, "Forgiveness is the willingness to have something happen the way it happened." What does this mean to you?

Week Three: Here Is Joy, Here Is Hope
Day 15: J. Barrie Shepherd uses the cup of wine as a symbol for the cup of "passion and of joy . . . the offering of life in love and service." What is the cup Jesus offers you this day? What is your response to that offer?

Day 16: The story of *Zorba* ends with two men dancing and celebrating life at the sight of their greatest failure. How does the Resurrection of Christ give you hope to celebrate in the face of seeming failure?

Day 17: For the author of this meditation, Anna White became a sign of resurrection life as she "danced the cross." How are *you* a sign of resurrection life?

Day 18: Read "Christ Comes Running" and personalize it as if it were you this encounter is happening to. How do you feel? Can you remember a time recently when you knew Christ was having a "holy party" on your behalf? Do you recognize your last "inch of growth"?

Day 19: Psalm 148 is a hymn of creation, inviting both heaven and earth to sing praise. What can you celebrate today? How have you noticed God at work today? Read Psalm 148 again for ideas.

Day 20: The author uses his abhorrence of war and yet continuing to pay war taxes as an example of his resistance to living "on the cross" with tension and contradiction. What "cross" do you resist now in your life? What did this article say to you about that tension?

Day 21: For the author of this meditation, his childhood hackberry tree provided a place of forgetting and avoidance. He compares God to that tree as a place of refuge. What is the difference between running away from your problems and running to God?

Week Four: Turning Toward God
Day 22: The author conveys her sense of uneasiness with the terms, "singleness of purpose" and "purity of heart"; they sometimes seem like "unattainable fantasies." In special moments with God, however, she understood their meanings more. What do these terms mean to you? Do they indicate perfection?

Day 23: The man in the story "Shadowbound" found a certain comfort in doing the same thing every day, but he also felt "trapped and alone." Listening and responding to the Voice changed his course completely. What is the message of this story for you? Can you identify with the man's uncertainty in trying a new direction? Explain.

Day 24: In writing about Psalm 139, Catherine Gunsalus González says that "God knows us better than we know ourselves." What is frightening about God's intimate knowledge of you? What is comforting about it?

Day 25: Like most of us, it took Richard a while to understand Bill's needs and to want to help him and be a friend. Is there someone you need to reach out to and "take under your wing"? What about a group or cause that you need to advocate for?

Day 26: The author talks about the two poles we experience within ourselves: one being the desire for transformation to the "best and truest self" we can be, and the other being fear of change and resistance to the new. Discuss your tension between longing for transformation and yet longing for the familiar.

Day 27: Richard Morgan writes that "we have to say goodbye to the old in order to say hello to the new." What in your life do you need to say goodbye to? What do you need to invite in with a big hello?

Day 28: Jean Blomquist writes that for many years she waited and wished for God to do *big* things in her life. Discuss her statement: "Instead of waiting for God to do big things in my life, I seek to dance in the embrace of the Holy One by fully encountering each marvelous, mundane moment."

Week Five: Love Beyond Understanding

Day 29: The therapist in this meditation experienced "transforming love" through her relationship with a sick and dying woman. Discuss an incident or relationship in which you have experienced God's transforming love.

Day 30: The author talks about his struggle to really love others and asks that his commitment to love be "more than good intentions." What is one way you can turn an inner commitment to love someone into action this week?

Day 31: Sam experienced a wrenching struggle with his decision of whether to go on to the game or to stop and help Augie-dog. When have you faced a decision in which there seemed to be no "best" answer? How did you resolve the decision?

Day 32: The author describes a long-term friendship and the comfort it brings—even though there may be times when he doesn't feel the need for the friendship. Are you this kind of friend to anyone? Who is this kind of friend to you?

Day 33: Gustavo Gutiérrez says that "The neighbor is not someone whom I find in my path but rather someone in whose path I place myself." In other words, you may have to go out of your way to actually see the needs of those who need you to be a neighbor. Who are the "distant ones" you need to draw close to through your commitment to love and serve them?

Day 34: In making a bed, the author found a deeper meaning to an everyday task. What are the little ways that you show your love through doing ordinary things every day? How do others show love for you in this way?

Day 35: The nineteen-year-old boy in this story experienced the persistence and care of those in his congregation after a decision to quit being involved in church. Discuss the author's statement: "Once God, through the church, has claimed us in baptism, God does not let us go easily."

Week Six: Times of Trial
Day 36: The woman in this meditation found a creative way to honor the memories of loved ones who had died, while reaching out to others. How can you be "mindful of those who aren't here" and "help those who are"?

Day 37: Psalm 130 is known as the classic penitential psalm: "Out of the depths I cry to you, O Lord." When in your life have you experienced these types of feelings? Why is it sometimes hard to be open to God's presence when you are in despair?

Day 38: Jean Blomquist describes a time in her life, her divorce, when it was very hard for her to feel the presence of God. Discuss her reference to the statement: "Tears are a sign of the presence of God."

Day 39: Rabbits grow fur as the temperature demands it. Discuss examples of "fur-growing" experiences when you or others gained the capacity to handle trouble.

Day 40: The author asserts that while we live in an age of alienation and loneliness, Jesus must have felt very lonely amid the crowd on Palm Sunday. Why would he have felt lonely? Have you ever felt lonely in the presence of others? Why?

Day 41: In the Garden of Gethsemane, Jesus struggled in prayer with God, searching for some other way through what he knew was ahead of him. Have you ever wished for an "escape hatch" from your life's situation? How do you handle those feelings?

Day 42: The writer of this meditation received personal insight into the reality of Christ's sacrifice for her. Can you remember a time when God's truth was made real to you? How did you respond?

Week Seven: Through the Darkness into the Light
Day 43: In this meditation, Judas Iscariot is portrayed as betraying Jesus for the sake of the cause, in order to further God's kingdom. What impression of Judas Iscariot do you get from this meditation? How is it different from your earlier impression of him?

Day 44: Barbara Brown Taylor talks about the good news and the bad news of being God's friends rather than God's servants. What is the "down side" of being God's friends? What do you think about Teresa of Avila's statement to God: "No wonder you have so few friends if this is how you treat them"?

Day 45: Read the crucifixion account in all the gospels to find the last words spoken by Jesus before his death. Write them down. Meditate on these words.

Day 46: Marjorie J. Thompson makes this statement in her meditation: "To recognize the Resurrection is to awake in a new kind of morning, one in which the bleak human landscape of sin seems more the fading dream than encompassing reality." Have you ever experienced this kind of perspective on life? Discuss the difference it would make in your life to have a "Resurrection perspective."

Day 47 (Easter): Kefa Sempangi's experience with the Nubian assassins made him feel as if he had passed from death to life. What does his article say to you about the power of prayer?

After Easter: Looking back on Holy Week, did you have a symbol or image that spoke to you in a personal way about Jesus' death and resurrection?

ABOUT THE AUTHORS

Phyllis Tickle is a poet and essayist who served for a number of years as the Director of St. Lukes Press and of the Trade Publishing Division of The Wimmer Companies. She resigned that position in 1991 in order to have more time for her own work.

Kenneth G. Phifer was senior minister of the St. Charles Avenue Presbyterian Church in New Orleans for eighteen years. He wrote *A Book of Uncommon Prayer* and most of the manuscript for *A Book of Uncommon Faith* before his death in 1985.

Larry R. Kalajainen is pastor of the United Methodist Church at New Brunswick, New Jersey, and has a Ph.D. in New Testament studies from Drew University Graduate School. The author is a member of the Society of Biblical Literature. He and his wife, Carol, served six years as World Division missionaries in Sarawak, East Malaysia.

Wanda M. Trawick is an announcer for Public Radio 89, WETS-FM, in Johnson City, Tennessee. She teaches an adult class at Watauga Avenue Presbyterian Church in Johnson City.

Bill Bates is senior pastor at First United Methodist Church in Fargo, North Dakota. He is married and has two teenagers.

Rueben P. Job, a retired United Methodist Bishop, is on the staff of The Upper Room working in the area of spiritual formation.

Anne Broyles is co-pastor of Malibu United Methodist Church in Malibu, California. She is author of *Journaling: A Spirit Journey* (Upper Room Books, 1988) and *Meeting God Through Worship* (Abingdon, 1992).

K. Cherie Jones is International Director of The Walk to Emmaus, a program of The Upper Room, Nashville, Tennessee.

Carole Chase, an ordained Presbyterian minister, was born and raised in the Panama Canal Zone. She earned her Ph.D. at Duke University and teaches religious studies at Elon College in North Carolina.

Helen R. Neinast is director of pastoral services at Charter Hospital of Pasco. She is a consultant and freelance writer in Land O' Lakes, Florida. She was formerly director of the Division of Higher Education at the Board of Higher Education and Ministry of The United Methodist Church. **Thomas C. Ettinger** is pastor of First United Methodist Church in Land O' Lakes, Florida. He has been pastor to several churches in Florida, and campus minister at Florida Atlantic University and Florida State University.

Flora Slosson Wuellner is a retreat leader, spiritual guide, and teacher. She is an ordained minister in the United Church of Christ and an internationally recognized author on the subjects of healing and spirituality. Her books include *Prayer, Stress, and Our Inner Wounds; Prayer and Our Bodies; Prayer, Fear and Our Powers,* and *Heart of Healing, Heart of Light.*

Mary Montgomery has written books and numerous short stories for young children and adolescents. She and her husband live in Edina, Minnesota. Their daughter and two sons are now young adults.

Pixie Koestline Hammond is a retired Methodist minister and a full-time seminar leader for the Foundation for Global Community in Palo Alto, California.

Thomas John Carlisle was a Presbyterian pastor and poet (1913-1992). His latest book of poetry, *The Living Word,* will be published posthumously by Eerdman's in the spring.

J. Barrie Shepherd is pastor of The First Presbyterian Church in the City of New York. Prior to this position, he was senior minister of Swarthmore Presbyterian Church in Swarthmore, Pennsylvania for sixteen years. He is the author of ten books, including *Seeing with the Soul* and *Faces at the Manger,* both published by Upper Room Books.

Maxie Dunnam is senior pastor of Christ United Methodist Church in Memphis, Tennessee. World Editor of The Upper Room from 1975 to 1982, Dr. Dunnam is widely known as an evangelism leader and a pioneer in small group ministries. Dr. Dunnam is the author of more than two dozen books and a popular series of workbooks on the Christian life.

Marilyn Wickel is a pastoral assistant at a parish in New Jersey. She also coordinates the Deaf Ministry in the Diocese of Metuchen.

Jim Frisbie is co-pastor of a new congregation in Chubbuck, Idaho. He wrote "Christ Comes Running" as part of a book of poems he wrote as a project while attending The Academy for Spiritual Formation. He has continued to write poems, articles, and short stories.

Donald E. Collins is pastor of the Church of the Good Hope, a United Methodist congregation in Milwaukee, Wisconsin. He has special interests in spiritual formation, worship, and ecumenism. He is the author of *Like Trees That Grow Beside a Stream* (Upper Room Books, 1991) and the forthcoming *The Kingdom of God Is in Your Midst* (Upper Room Books, 1993).

Parker J. Palmer is an independent author, speaker, and activist who lives in Madison, Wisconsin. His books include *The Active Life, The Company of Strangers,* and *To Know As We Are Known.*

Beth A. Richardson is a diaconal minister and assistant editor of *alive now!* magazine, published by The Upper Room, Nashville, Tennessee.

David M. Griebner is a United Methodist minister currently serving Riverside United Methodist Church in Columbus, Ohio. He studied spiritual guidance through Shalem Institute for Spiritual Formation in Washington, D.C. He is married and has three daughters.

Lois Duffield and her husband own an environmental consulting business in Guilford, Connecticut.

Catherine Gunsalus González is Professor of Church History at Columbia Theological Seminary in Decatur, Georgia.

Richard L. Whitaker is Diaconal Minister of Christian Education at the Whitefish Bay United Methodist Church in Wisconsin. The story, "Do I Have to Take Him with Me?" occurred over thirty years ago in his home church, Epworth United Methodist Church, in Savannah, Georgia.

John S. Mogabgab is the editor of *Weavings: A Journal of the Christian Spiritual Life*. He is a member of the Ecumenical Institute of Spirituality and has led many retreats and workshops on the spiritual life.

Richard L. Morgan is the Older Adult Enabler for the Presbytery of Western North Carolina and editor of *Agenda,* published by the Presbyterian Church (USA). In his retirement he serves as Supply Minister of the Presbyterian Church of Spindale, North Carolina, where he intends to initiate an Older Adult Ministry for eight churches in the county.

Jean M. Blomquist is a writer whose work focuses primarily on spirituality and contemporary religious issues. She and her husband live in Berkeley, California.

Gerry H. Moore is a writer of short stories and lives in Grand Junction, Colorado. In addition to writing, she has been a wife, mother, teacher, bowling lanes co-proprietor, real estate agent, and grandmother.

Gustavo Gutiérrez is a professor in the department of theology and social sciences in the Catholic Pontifical University in Lima, Peru. He became internationally known in the 1970s with the publication of his first major book, *Theologia de la liberatión*.

Dorothy Hanson Brown is a veteran writer for radio and television and has also been producer and talent for both media. She has been a frequent contributor to *alive now!* for the past fourteen years. She had her husband, Harold, live in Snyder, New York, and have four grown children.

William H. Willimon is Dean of the Chapel and Professor of Christian Ministry at Duke Divinity School in Durham, North Carolina. He has written several books for Upper Room Books, including *Remember Who You Are, Sunday Dinner,* and *With Glad and Generous Hearts.*

Donna Schaper is a writer, farmer, and pastor in Riverhead, New York. She is also the mother of three young farmers, one of whom belongs to a rabbit club.

Donald J. Shelby is senior minister at First United Methodist Church in Santa Monica, California. He has written *Meeting the Messiah, Forever Beginning,* and *The Unsettling Season.*

James A. Harnish is senior pastor at Hyde Park United Methodist Church in Tampa, Florida. Prior to this position he spent thirteen years as pastor at St. Luke's United Methodist Church in Orlando. He has written four books published by Upper Room Books; his latest is *God Isn't Finished with Us Yet.*

Barbara Seaman is a fourth generation Kansan and a graduate of Wheaton College. Her poetry has appeared in many Christian and literary journals.

Mary Lou Redding is the managing editor of *The Upper Room* Daily Devotional Guide. She is a writer, and workshop and retreat leader in Nashville, Tennessee.

Barbara Brown Taylor is rector of Grace-Calvary Church in Clarkesville, Georgia. Her most recent book, *The Preaching Life,* is forthcoming from Cowley Publications in 1993.

Ken Fansler is a retired United Methodist minister living in Nashville, Tennessee. He is a freelance writer and enjoys teaching elderhostel courses.

Marjorie J. Thompson is a Presbyterian minister, teacher, writer, and retreat leader in the area of Christian spiritual formation. She is the author of *Family: The Forming Center* and lives in Goodlettsville, Tennessee.

Michael E. Williams is one of the pastors at Belle Meade United Methodist Church in Nashville, Tennessee, and general editor of *The Storyteller's Companion to the Bible* series (Abingdon).

Kenneth L. Gibble is co-pastor with his wife, Ann, of the Arlington Church of the Brethren in Arlington, Virginia. His most recent book is *Once Upon a Wonder: Imaginings from the Gospels* published by Upper Room Books.

Ron DelBene is an Episcopal priest, author, spiritual director, and retreat leader. He has written the *Into the Light* series, *Christmas Remembered, From the Heart,* and *The Breath of Life* series.

Readings
for
Lent and Easter